Making Poems

Making Poems

Forty Poems with Commentary by the Poets

Edited by
Todd Davis
and
Erin Murphy

excelsior editions

State University of New York Press
Albany, New York

COVER ART: "Casita Window, New Mexico, 2005" by Nancy Rumfield (photograph)

"Red Sugar is from *Red Sugar* by Jan Beatty, © 2008, and is reprinted here by permission of the University of Pittsburgh Press. "Man of the Year" is from *Domain of Perfect Affection*, by Robin Becker, © 2006, and is reprinted here by permission of the University of Pittsburgh Press.

Published by State University of New York Press, Albany

For information, contact State University of New York Press, Albany, NY
www.sunypress.edu

Production by Kelli W. LeRoux
Marketing by Fran Keneston

Library of Congress Cataloging-in-Publication Data

Making poems : forty poems with commentary by the poets / [edited by] Todd Davis, Erin Murphy.
    p. cm.
  ISBN 978-1-4384-3175-8 (hardcover : alk. paper) — ISBN 978-1-4384-3176-5 (pbk. : alk. paper) 1. American poetry—21st century. 2. American poetry—20th century. 3. Poetry—Authorship. 4. Creative writing. I. Davis, Todd, 1965–
II. Murphy, Erin, 1968–
  PS617.M36 2010
  811'.608—dc22

808.81
MAK

                                                                    2009040359

10 9 8 7 6 5 4 3 2 1

For Shelly and Rich and all of our students

Contents

Contents

Contents

Contents

Learning To Make Poems—
An Introduction

Poetry is when an emotion has found its thought and the thought has found words.
—ROBERT FROST

The poet doesn't invent. He listens.
—JEAN COCTEAU

No one can tell you how best to make the writing happen. For one poet at least, short naps have proved helpful; for him, leaving consciousness for a brief time is invitational to the inner, "poetic" voice. For myself, walking works in a similar way. I walk slowly and not to get anywhere in particular, but because the motion somehow helps the poem to begin. I end up, usually, standing still, writing something down in the small notebook I always have with me.
—MARY OLIVER

Poetry is just the evidence of life. If your life is burning well, poetry is just the ash.
—LEONARD COHEN

What makes a poem a poem, finally, is that it is unparaphrasable. There is no other way to say exactly this; it exists only in its own body of language, only in these words.
—MARK DOTY

> *First having read the book of myths,*
> *and loaded the camera,*
> *and checked the edge of the knife-blade,*
> *I put on*
> *the body-armor of black rubber*
> *the absurd flippers*
> *the grave and awkward mask.*
> *I am having to do this*
> *not like Cousteau with his*
> *assiduous team*
> *aboard the sun-flooded schooner*
> *but here alone.*
> —ADRIENNE RICH

WHERE EXACTLY do poems come from? On rare occasions they seem to materialize with an immediacy akin to enchantment. At other times, it's exceedingly clear that they are the product of painstaking and arduous commitment to failure after failure until out of the wreckage some semblance of a poem appears. More often than not, however, they seem simply to be the result of daily activity—reading and thinking, scribbling and revising. The question of how poems come into being has puzzled practitioners and readers of the art since time in memoriam. And while many have cited the nebulous "muse," such an answer seems inadequate in the face of the radically different paths many poets have taken toward the writing of verse.

Whether teaching in the classroom, giving a reading, or casually conversing with friends and family, the most common question we encounter is: How do you write a poem? Implicit in this question is the puzzlement most of us have when we read a poem that *feels* right, that *sends* us in a direction we hadn't thought possible before entering the front door of the poem. At the back door, as we exit this house made of words, we wonder how it was constructed and whether the builder ever finds herself at a loss, too exhausted to consider taking on another poetry-construction project.

Certainly poetry can be about vision and inspiration, about some emotional or spiritual epiphany that sends us careening toward art as a means of expression. But if it were merely about such ecstatically fleeting moments, about hearing the song the muse sings, then the burgeoning floodwaters of inspiration might have drowned us in poems long ago; or, conversely, perhaps there would have been a dearth of poems, an artistic drought to end all droughts—for how many of us can claim the muse visits us as frequently as we wish?

The poets in this anthology have been asked to explore one of their own poems or the poetic process, to attempt to tell us how poems are born, explaining not only poetry's gestation and birth, but also the parenting that follows, the revisions that help move poetry toward independence and finally into the world of publication.

While some books on the craft of writing poems insinuate that there is a set of basic guidelines that "good" poets follow, the reality is much murkier. In our own exploration of this art form, we have discovered that each writer has his or her own patterns of behavior, his or her own liturgy or training schedule. And like most patterns of behavior, the anomalies—when the individual departs from his or her routine—sometime produce the most interesting results.

Of course, as Dan Gerber contends, poets often don't know how their poems come into being, but they can make valuable and sometimes important discoveries in the stories they make up, after the fact, about how a particular poem might have entered this world. The very act of explaining or re-creating how a poem is written is itself an act of creation. (Doesn't the writer always start from the beginning, attempting to make over—for what feels like the very first time—the poem, the story, the very means by which word will be placed next to word, image next to image, living tissue serving as mortar?)

As we enter the vision of each poet in this volume, we may be surprised at what we find—enlivened by how certain poems mirror our own existence, instructed in certain methods of revision or drafting, inspired to take a different path that diverges from the worn patterns of our own writing. One thing is certain: we will not be disappointed with the poems that have been made and the stories about their making; we will begin to have a deeper understanding of the complexity of human endeavor, at the way art is made and remade as a means of understanding all the poems that comprise our lives.

Jan Beatty

Red Sugar

You walk inside yourself on roads and ropes
of blood vessels and tendons, you walk inside
yourself and eat weather
  —GRETEL EHRLICH

When I was young, I was a comet
with an unending shimmering tail,
and I flew over the brokenness below
that was my life. I didn't know until I was
twelve that we carry other bodies inside us.
Not babies, but bodies of blood
that speak to us in plutonic languages
of pith and serum. When I was
six, there was a man in the woods,
naked. I didn't know him, but I knew
he was a wrong kind of man/so I ran.
With my inside body I see his skinny
white bones and curled mouth, he looks
like sickness and it's the body inside me
that's running, my red sugar body
that shows me the brutal road to love,
the one good man, the one song
I can keep as mine. I heard it once
when I was waitressing, something

made me turn my head, made me
swivel to look at a woman across
the room, wasn't even my station,
but the red sugar said, *go.* When I
saw her up close, I knew she was
blood. I can't explain this—I only met
my mother once. I said, *Do you know
a woman named Dorothy?* Her face
was pale, she said, *No*—in that hard way.
Maybe her red sugar told her to run—
but before she left, she grabbed my arm,
said, *I did have a sister named Dorothy,
but she died.* Two inches away from her
dyed blond hair, I said, *okay,* but both
our inside bodies knew she was lying.
Some people call it *eating weather*—
the way you swallow what you know,
but keep it—later it rises like a storm
from another world, reptilian and hungry.
It's the thickness that drives us and
stains us, the not asking/just coming/
the cunt alive and jewel-like/the uncut
garnet and the lava flow/it's barbarism/
bloodletting/the most liquid part of us/
spilling/spreading/the granular red sea
of sap and gore/sinking/moving forward
at the same time/slippery/red
containing blue/it's the sweet,
deep inside of the body.

FINDING "RED SUGAR"

"Red Sugar" was born in Wyoming, and its wildness was born inside and outside of the body of the poem. I had been trying to write a poem that was thick and gooey with the physicality of the body while at the same time invoking a kind of knowing that seemed inexplicable. I couldn't find the poem.

I was deep in a fight with myself about how to access the inside knowing of the body, the voices that drive us, and how to write about it. I had been writing narratives that were too linear for the subject. What story could I tell as a way to fully involve the body's messaging system, something that felt both mysterious and palpable?

At the time, I was staying at Jentel, an artist residency in Banner, Wyoming, in the Lower Piney Creek Valley. We could see the Big Horn Mountains from our studios. This was summer, 2003, when the planet Mars was drawing closer to Earth than it had been in recorded history. It would move to a position, according to scientists, of 34.65 million miles (55.76 million kilometers) away from Earth on August 27, 2003. Earth and Mars would be on the same side of the Sun (if seen from above); all three lined up in a row. This configuration, when Mars is in opposition, happens about every twenty-six months, but this particular event was different because the farthest part of Earth's orbit from the Sun (its aphelion) lined up with the closest part of Mars' orbit to the Sun (its perihelion). I don't pretend to know all the astronomical details, but I know that something happened at Jentel that late July, and it had everything to do with Mars. I don't want to sound superstitious or precious in my rendering, but I somehow have to tell you how Mars got into my poem, my body, the work of every artist in Piney Creek Valley. How else to say it: *We all turned red.*

It started with a lot of restlessness, which is common at residencies, with everyone converging on one place, urgent to do their work and unwind from their lives. There was an intensity there; a few clashes of personalities (also common), a sense of danger and heat, and then the rattlesnake sign over the kitchen sink: Rattlesnake by the Writer Studios. Put Boots On. I decided to work in my bedroom that night, staying up to all hours, finding myself writing lists of body parts. A lot of psychic disturbance was in the air. All of this, of course, can happen at an artist residency easily enough. Then the red started showing up. I started working on a poem called "Lip," started looking up synonyms for *red*, and making long lists. I put on Jimi Hendrix, listening to "Voodoo Child" over and over: "I'm standing next to a mountain / chop it down / with the edge of my hand. . . ."

That night I visited Rebecca, a painter from Santa Cruz. All over, and I mean all over her studio, were huge, blood-red calla lilies—painting after painting. All red. I stared as she said: "Do you think they're too much? I can't help myself, I just keep painting red; that's all I can do." I told her about my body parts list, my red list, my Hendrix revival, and she said that Beth, another painter, was obsessing about red also. "Do you think it's Mars?" she asked, and we walked outside to look. Nothing like the big Wyoming sky, and we didn't know which one was Mars, where to even look. We decided to talk to the other residents. And it grew. Everyone was feeling the restlessness; a few were feeling a pull towards something, and a few days later, the bleeding happened. There were five women artists there and one man at the time, and all the women who were still menstruating started bleeding.

We leaned into it. We started wearing red, writing red, painting red alive. Rebecca drove into Buffalo and brought me a swatch of deep red material that I hung in my studio. Another artist bought me a vintage toy—a red motorcycle for my writing room. We couldn't wait for the evenings to look at the sky and talk about the work that was rising up. On one of those nights, "Red Sugar" was born. I started out, "When I was young . . ." and then something about growing up. But it wasn't right; it wasn't diving deep enough. I remember looking at the sky from my writing studio and something breaking loose: "When I was young, I was a comet." I thought, *Can I say this?* And then, line 2: "with an unending shimmering tail." I felt things starting to break away: lines 3 and 4: "and I flew over the brokenness below / that was my life." That was it! I needed to fly, to be a celestial body flying over the earthly body, and all of this Mars fire, this red lily/women bleeding/ Hendrix fire was necessary to get me there. After that beginning, I was able to get to the rolling story of the body in the poem: ". . . a storm/from another world, reptilian and hungry. It's the thickness that drives us and/stains us, the not asking/just coming/the cunt alive and jewel-like/the uncut/garnet and the lava flow. . . ."

Could I have found "Red Sugar," the comet, the sky, the plutonic languages of the poem without Mars, without the "red" of it? I was trying to talk about the bodies inside and outside of us, which now seemed to include the bodies of planets, the bodies of the other artists, the body of the mountain in the dark, bodies of light in the night sky. It would take me days after that to write the end, the thick and gooey red list: ". . . it's barbarism/bloodletting/the most liquid part of us/spilling/spreading/the granular red sea/of sap and gore /sinking/moving forward/at the same time/slippery/red/containing blue/it's the sweet,/deep inside of the body."

Man of the Year

My father tells the story of his life,

and he repeats *The most important thing:*
    to love your work.
I always loved my work. I was a lucky man.

This man who makes up half of who I am,
    this blusterer
who tricked the rich, outsmarting smarter men,

gave up his Army life insurance plan
    (not thinking of the future
wife and kids) and brokered deals with two-faced

rats who disappeared his cash but later overpaid
    for building sites. In every tale
my father plays outlaw, a Robin Hood

for whom I'm named, a type of yeoman thug
    refused admission
into certain clubs. For years he joined no guild—

no *Drapers, Goldsmiths, Skinners, Merchant
    Tailors, Salters, Vintners*—
but lived on prescience and cleverness.

He was the self-inventing Polish immigrant's
    son, transformed
by American tools into Errol Flynn.

As he speaks, I remember the phone calls
    during meals—
an old woman dead in apartment two-twelve

or burst pipes and water flooding rooms.
    Hatless,
he left the house and my mother's face

assumed the permanent worry she wore,
    forced to watch him
gamble the future of the semi-detached house,

our college funds, his weekly payroll.
    Manorial halls
of Philadelphia his Nottingham,

my father fashioned his fraternity
    without patronage
or royal charters but a mercantile

swagger, finding his Little John, Tinker,
    and Allen-a-Dale.
Wholesalers, retailers, in time they resembled

the men they set themselves against.
    Each year they roast and toast
one member, a remnant of the Grocer's Feast

held on St. Anthony's Day, when brothers
    communed and dined
on swan, capon, partridges, and wine.

They commission a coat of arms, a song,
    and honor my father—
exemplary, self-made, without debt—

as Man of the Year, a title he reveres
    for the distinguished
peerage he joins, the lineage of merry men.

STRANGE TERCETS:
MERRY MEN, IAMBIC FEET, AND POETIC TRANSGRESSION

Many poems spring from the desire to understand our origins. Poems that probe a speaker's literal and metaphorical sources or explore family dynamics fascinate us. I'm partial to poems that examine sibling relationships and have collected quite a few over the years. In writing about my family of origin, I've employed diverse geographical and historical material to find the imagery and sensory detail that suit a particular poem and carry it from the private into the public realm.

As a writer who uses autobiographical material to catalyze a poem, I must be especially careful to edit out what literally happened when that information has meaning only to me. Thus, I'm always alert to the apt simile or metaphor that might mirror or reconfigure or enlarge upon the merely factual. Some examples: my mother is a Leni Lenape in a poem called "The Poconos"; at poem's close, she barters "her freedom/for a modest home on a small tract of land." In "Borderline," the speaker views her sister as an organism struggling to adapt and survive in the salt- and freshwater environment of an estuary: "Neither barrier beach/nor tide pool nor undersea meadow/could nourish you."

Poets constantly make decisions about the prosody of poems. What diction suits this speaker? What kinds of sentences will build a dynamic, syntactical tension? How do we wish the poem to look on the page? Long lines? Short lines? Stanza shape? How might internal rhyme unify the tropes? Should descriptive material originate in the same image-hoard? What allusions, literary or otherwise, deepen the poem's capacities?

Obscure or popular, myths and legends supply writers with characters enacting life's dramas, exhibiting flaws and strengths in vivid stories that sometimes cross cultures. In "Man of the Year," I wanted to depict the speaker's father in his complexity: selfish and canny, immigrant's son and successful rogue. I struggled to cull useful true details, even as I searched for a fictional context. Since childhood, I've been fascinated by the legend of Robin Hood and his band living in Sherwood Forest. With other kids on my block in Philadelphia, we playacted the Merry Men, Maid Marion, and Little John, donning green leotards and fashioning quivers. Years later, I researched the legend and read about medieval and Renaissance outlaw narratives, the focus on exile, justice, legal authority, and its rupture. I considered the homosocial aspects of the legend and its celebration of transgressive behaviors. I studied the history of English guilds and their membership practices. For years, I saved this material in a file. One day, working on "Man of the Year," I discovered that I could employ some of the imagery in my poem.

"My father tells the story of his life" provides the opening framing device within which the semi-chronological narrative unfolds. The father's self-portrait—I always loved my work. I was a lucky man—quickly gives way to the speaker's portrait of her father as "this blusterer/who tricked the rich, outsmarting smarter men." Two stanzas later, Robin Hood appears, followed by Errol Flynn, star of the 1938 film *The Adventures of Robin Hood* and a popular swashbuckling hero. I decided to try to interweave contemporary and legendary details, creating a hybrid character both reckless and risk-taking, beloved by his fellows, admired and resented by his family. After assembling all of my research into medieval and early modern periods, I ended up using only bits of information, such as the names of several English guilds and the foods served at the annual, all-male Grocer's Feast on St. Anthony's Day.

In thinking about how I wanted the poem to look on the page, I considered how its form might best mirror content and theme. The poem concerns the shaping of a life story, the tools we use to give inchoate biographical details a meaningful container, or form. The (lucky) iambic pentameter of the opening line—"My father tells the story of his life"—set me up. I experimented with all iambic lines and found them too regular for the entire poem; they did, however, create a recognizable rhythm against which I could work. I nixed couplets and quatrains as too neat. Having recently read Linda Gregerson's *The Woman Who Died in Her Sleep* and admired her "unbalanced" tercets, I tried to use the briefer, inverted mid-line to give the poem movement and bring some air into a poem dense with images and music.

I revised and revised to find sounds that crackled and rang out against each other. I sought long vowel sounds and single-syllable words with hard consonants, such as *rats* and *tricked*. Single-word repetition (work), slant rhyme (tools/calls/meals and reveres/peerage/lineage) and scattered slant end-rhyme (am/men, payroll/Manorial halls, /against/toast/feast) lent the poem a surprising music. Alliteration helped unify diction ("father fashioned his fraternity"). I combined end-stopped with run-on lines, and only four stanzas concluded with periods to emphasize the brisk pace of "Man of the Year." Many lines contain ten or eleven syllables, the extra syllable emphasizing the unstable quality of the character's work life. In revising, I tried to begin and end lines on important words such as *mercantile* and *swagger*. Finally, I cut the last two stanzas of the poem, which, in the earlier version, shifted the focus from the father to the daughter. The commentary included in those last six lines cluttered the poem with interpretation, as if the speaker couldn't trust the reader to understand the poem's intentions. Now, the poem ends with a celebration of peerage among men. Readers may do what they wish with that.

Fleda Brown

Knot Tying Lessons: The Slip Knot
—the most useful temporary knot or noose

What can I say? I turned a corner. No matter
that I doubled back, there was still progress. I was lying
low, crossing under both my coming and going,
and when I rose to see where I was, felt the cool
air on my face, I skidded like a skater, wrapped around
myself again, burrowing back up through the small
figure-eight I'd made of myself. How secure it all seemed,
how sure to result in something unfaltering—patriotic,
even. But the way things have gone, I'm left with
a looseness through the center. I have loved well,
haven't I, and hard? But there's been this tendency to
let things drop. It's the opposites I have trouble with,
the way my attention begins expanding as if
the richness has eased past the borders, no longer
lives in this constriction, this lump in my throat.
I drew you to me with such firmness, you were sure
of the implications. The exact point at which I began
to be disappointed, who knows? The more I gave myself
room to work it out, the more I felt the movement
of possibilities within me. I should have felt relieved
when all fell through, but I only felt what I am,
how I'm made. "Open your mouth," my mother used to

11

say, coming at me with a bar of soap because of some
word I'd said. I opened, as I do now, willing to take
the bitterness, to have done what I did.

THE KNOT OF THE POEM

I'm by myself at the lake. It is October, very cool already, and I have a fire
going in the woodstove. The woodstove is older than I am, the damper is
almost gone, and there's a crack between the stove and the chimney that I
stuff with aluminum foil to keep the smoke from coming out into the room.
But I'm happy. I'm on sabbatical for the year and alone in my favorite place in
the world. In the little green cottage there's one bedroom, one bathroom, a
kitchen, and a living-dining area. I've always liked small spaces—they're
secure and controllable. I even like the hardship, the broken stove, the mess of
my father's sailboat rig stacked in the corner that I have to step around. To be
here alone with my computer, a few bottles of wine, and food so that I don't
have to go to the store for days makes me feel safe, drives me into my own in-
terior. I have stopped by the tiny local library and checked out a book of
knots, thinking that I'd like to write some poems about tying knots. My
father the sailor has always had the right knot at his disposal when needed,
but I can only tie a granny knot. Now that I have the cottage to take care of,
this is increasingly a problem. I need to hold a boat to shore, tie a tarp over
the pile of dock sections in the yard for the winter. If I learn to tie the knots
and get some poems out of it, all the better.

I try using a piece of shoestring to practice with. Too short. I fish around
in drawers and find a decent section of rope. I use a chair leg to tie to. I'm bad
at this. I'm dexterous, but I have a poor memory. I tie and re-tie and pull
apart a dozen times before I have the first one, a simple slipknot. I feel awk-
ward and stupid, like a child. Okay, I follow the knot in my mind as I make
each turn. I try to feel its movements. I am the slipknot. How have I slipped?
I have tried so hard to hold things together. I remained in two marriages that
should have slipped away years before they did. I circled, held and pulled, but
they inevitably slipped. So, is this the poem? Not yet. I have no idea where
the poem is yet. I begin with motion. I use the movements of tying the knot
to lead me. Slip knot? I like the way it makes itself out of itself, the way it
makes a loop, then goes through its own loop. It seems secure. But the nature
of this particular looping is to slip out when pulled. This both pleases and
upsets me. It's a magic trick, the slipping. The knot's gone in a second, pulled
apart from itself. I have identified myself with the knot, and now I'm aware of
the fear, the guilt, the slippage of my life when I passionately wanted to hold

it steady. The "you" in the poem? Oh, this poem wants to defend me, explain me, to someone.

This is a formula, these directions for a knot. This poem is more sure than I am, which is a comfort. It is a rope. It is assured in its rope-ness; it is what it is. I have separated from it at some point. It's all true of me, the willingness to take the bitterness. I don't regret what I've done, but the poem feels like a knot, like the knot that is this life I've had to slip out of, to live.

The voice in the poem has turned out not to be mine, surely. It is more casual, more cool about the slippage. It is the voice of the snaky rope. When it says it's tried hard, I don't believe it. I think it knew all along it was a slipknot. What did it feel when all fell through? Nothing, it says. Only, like Popeye, that "I yam what I yam."

How did the poem take on this voice? I remember the horror of feeling—both times—that I'd made a mistake, that I was smothering in the marriage, the sudden awareness that I didn't love him. This is the driving energy in the poem, that horror of that moment, when I wanted to love, when I wanted to be what I said I would be when I made the vows. But the impetus was uncontrollably away. And beneath the struggle, the pain, and the sadness, the bare truth was that the line of my life was going to go where it went.

I was happy to arrive at the image of my mother washing out my mouth with soap. That came later, as I revised, as I was looking for a way back to earth. The poem had been harmonizing human and rope-voice as perfectly as I could make it do. That voice seemed to me eerie, unreal. I needed to raise the human voice up, let the rope voice soften at the end, almost out of hearing. The poem is about people, not ropes.

This poem owes to Whitman its need to expose all, even the worst. It owes to Whitman the rope's way of forgiving itself for being what it is. It owes to our recent government (George W. Bush's voice surely slipped into the poem) the voice of the self-assured "patriotic" rope. It owes to my upbringing its determined rationality, its upright shape, its need to argue the point convincingly. Heaven knows who else it owes: all the poets who've been willing to stick with cause and effect to see what to make of their dance.

J. L. Conrad

Brother André's Heart: Montreal, 2003

In 1973, the heart gone, pilgrims
climb the stairs on knees to eye

the heartless man in his hollow chamber.
Memory's plumbline laid from there to here

on limestone. The mountain around which the city.
Yes, I remember. A new opening

through which the body remade itself.
Rocks knocked from mountainsides

brought here to bear weight upward until
even the impression of weight lifts off into

the recessed darkness pooled beneath the roof.
We stand in the votive chapel six days married.

A bank of candles: whipstitch of lights
sealing the wound. Columns bristle

with rows of crutches. We do not yet know
how bodies cave, how bones surface. We take

15

no pictures. No, that's not true.
We take two: one into the washed-out summer

sky. Me wearing sunglasses, the carved
angel rising behind my shoulder. And another

on surfacing from the crypt, sun breaking
into pieces, rimming each edge with light.

See how clouds cut into the sky.
See how the geese are black slashes

unstitching the firmament. Beyond
the open door, the heart lies suspended

in a jar, bathed in a red heatlamped glow.
The papers reported it found

in an empty apartment locked in a box
inside another box. How they must

have wrenched it from the body.
You've remembered it wrong

all these years: the jagged undoing,
snipping each stitch so the wound gapes open

again. Today, pilgrims file past the vault
in silence: my body parched, yours

stationed there beside me,
on the near side of desire. Holy water laid

between us. In what voice do I
call out? A brittle light, hearts sundered.

We can't be blamed if things come apart.
We can scarcely be accused of theft. What we take

we take from each other. Our dreams wearing horns
like sacrificial rams. We know in our bones,

which is to say our deepest selves, the world
thrown open, the veil torn, seeded fields ungrown

at last. It falls to us to shovel dirt over the flames.
Sometimes, they say, the heart still beats.

We did not ask for this. The one day a year
wine becomes unsettled, remembering.

TENEBRAE: LIVING IN/AMONG SHADOWS

July 4, 2003: My husband and I are in Montreal for the last leg of our honeymoon. We've spent the week walking, taking in the sights.

This morning, as each morning before, we wake and take breakfast in the yellow dining room with its Moroccan lanterns. We eat passion fruit mousse and drink fresh-squeezed orange juice. The heat stifles breath, draws thick into lungs. Air enfolds the city like arms.

Mont Royal, which gives the city its name, lies north of downtown. St. Joseph's Oratory (Oratoire Saint-Joseph) rises dramatically from its northwestern slope. The basilica is impressive; its dome the second-largest in the world. For years, Brother André (born Alfred Bessette) tended the sick there, ministering to them with oil from the lamp burning at the feet of St. Joseph's statue. As his reputation as a healer spread, pilgrims flocked to see him. The oratory is the culmination of a lifetime of labor; although Brother André, who died in 1937 at the age of 91, did not live to see its completion, his body and heart now reside within its walls.

To reach the oratory, we follow a circuitous path. I wear new sandals that do not fit. Because they chafe, I take them off while crossing the expanse of grass leading up to the oratory. At the stairs cut into the hill, we pause. It does not seem possible to go any further in the heat. We've brought no water with us. Inside, we find a holy water machine where small bottles can be

17

purchased and filled. I buy one and rub some of the water into a damp film on my hot arms and face. It seems to help.

There are few pictures from our honeymoon. One, taken into the mirror in our room, shows me blurred, features illegible, and a light shining strongly from behind. Another is taken at the oratory, where we surface onto a terrace overlooking the city, the sky bold and unexpected. Clouds obscure the sun, their edges limned with light.

Afterwards, we visit the small chapel on the hill: the first offering place, its walls lined with crutches. That evening we eat in a small Cajun restaurant. We are the only people present except for the owner, who cooks us a feast of fish, cornbread, and soup.

What else? It is our honeymoon. We wander the city feeling—what? Blessed is the wrong word. Each step taken seems somehow detached: my body unfamiliar and light.

⚭

Skip ahead four years. I have begun meeting with a poetry group. One of the other poets bases her writing on meticulous research of places. I decide to try her method.

In the process of investigating St. Joseph's Oratory, I come across news reports that Brother André's heart had been stolen. (Even now, no one knows who accomplished the theft or how.) The heart remained missing from March 1973 to December 1974, when an anonymous caller tipped off the police to its whereabouts.

Hearts and their associations with violence fascinate me. One of the legends of St. Valentine, for instance, recounts that the night before he was executed, he wrote letters to his friends telling them how much he cared. The next day, he was beheaded.

Love and violence seem inextricably intertwined.

In "Brother André's Heart," I am thinking about stitching: the way two lives are stitched into one, the way threads sometimes seal wounds when skin cannot hold itself. When young, I suffered a facial injury that made me sure I would never be loved. When you are fourteen, you believe the mirror and what it tells you. I saw a girl with a lash of black threads holding her face together. I saw a girl with an angry pink scar. I saw something whole sundered.

Meeting my husband was a slow unfolding—an opening up like plants to rain. He sent me a heart cookie by mail for Valentine's Day.

The evening he proposed, we walked a breakwater from one side to the other on the tip of furled land that is Cape Cod. Threads of lightning sundered the sky in the distance. We were the tallest things for miles. "Shouldn't we turn back?" I asked again and again. At the end we stopped. The sky lay heavy and waiting.

18

☙

What else can I say about the poem?

I believe in scavenging from other poems. And worrying images until they emerge in the right place. The idea of geese as black slashes, for instance, appeared as early as 1999 in a poem that never came to fruition. There I wrote of "birds—/black scars overhead."

The poem also describes a "carved angel rising behind my shoulder." Now that I think about it, I suppose I actually lied in writing this line.

"Brother André's Heart" considers change, the now between before and after, the possibilities for violence and healing that lie plangent and ready to burst into each moment. The sudden turning: the touching of the garment's hem. We tremble in anticipation of what will come.

Sometimes we can see past the wreckage into something urgent, glimmering, ripe with meaning. If only we could grasp it.

The poem's last line, "The one day a year wine becomes unsettled, remembering," refers to a belief a friend related to me several years ago: wine in the bottle becomes, on the anniversary of its separation from the mother vine, unfit to drink. Memory, I like to think, sometimes exists at a cellular level.

We cannot ever truly see each other. Yet we catch glimpses.

I still have the holy water.

Jim Daniels

Factory Jungle

Right after the seven o'clock break
the ropes start shining down,
thin light through the factory windows,
the sun on its way to the time clock.
My veins fill with welding flux—
I get that itchy feeling I don't belong here.

I stand behind the biggest press in the plant
waiting for the parts to drop down into the rack,
thinking about what that mad elephant
could do to a hand.

I'd like to climb one of those ropes of light
swing around the plant
between presses, welders, assembly lines
past the man working the overhead crane
everyone looking up, swearing off booze, pills,
whatever they think made them see me.
I'd shed my boots, coveralls, safety glasses, ear plugs,
and fly out the plant gate
past the guard post
and into the last hour of twilight.

The parts are backing up
but I don't care.
I rip open my coveralls and pound my chest
trying to raise my voice
above the roar of the machines
yelling louder than Tarzan ever had to.

OK FOR SHIPMENT

I worked the afternoon shift, three to eleven, at the Ford Sterling Axle Plant in Sterling Heights, Michigan, in the summer of 1978. The area I worked in was called High Bay because the ceilings were higher than in the rest of the plant in order to accommodate a large overhead crane that moved back and forth across the ceiling, moving large rolls of steel and the dyes for the punch presses. It was the only area in the plant that had windows, up high near the crane. Every night around 7 PM., if the sun was out, it shone through those windows on its way to setting. It was the contrast between darkness and light, between stillness and movement, between safety and danger, that I think prompted me to rip off a green quality control OK for Shipment tag from a basket of parts and scribble "jungle idea—grabbing onto rays of light" and stuff it in my pocket. I'm not sure what happened to that basket of parts. I once saw a foreman rip off a Rejected tag and attach an OK tag to a basket to help make his production quota for the day; in comparison, I feel I can justify my small crime in the name of poetry.

When I first sat down some months later to try to expand that note into a poem, I focused on the simple jungle metaphor. The rays of light were very long and thin, almost tangible, reminding me of vines hanging down from trees in a jungle Also, as suggested by these safety posters on display in the plant, the factory was incredibly noisy (Hearing Protection Required) and dangerous (Daydreams Can Cause Nightmares, Eyes: Only Two to a Customer) The factory was full of wires and conveyors for the assembly-line process, and the paths between machines were often narrow. In a strange way, the whole landscape resembled the thick underbrush of a jungle. In fact, I had not ever been in a jungle; so where did I get these ideas of what a jungle was like? Tarzan movies.

The first draft of the poem was almost haiku-like in its structure and brevity, with four lines establishing the image of the light shining in, and three lines describing my personal connection to the image: ". . . every day/I feel like grabbing one of those beams/and swinging through the plant." Already, the imagistic core of the poem was there in the visual contrast between light and dark, and the emotional core was there also—the idea of wanting to get away from the monotony of the work, of escaping into an imaginary world where those rays would be sturdy enough to swing away on.

What *wasn't* there was the physical environment of the plant—that was all still in my head. The draft was still more like a sketch for a poem than a poem, petering out with that statement about wanting to swing through the plant. The next draft worked to bring the factory into the poem, along with my place in the factory: "as I stood behind the presses waiting for the parts to drop down." In addition, figurative language started creeping in which also used the physical setting of the factory: ". . . the blood/flowed through my veins/like welding flux/I'd get that itchy feeling that I don't belong here." Welding flux was very itchy if it got on your skin, and I was using it to get at my longing for escape. The next draft added a metaphor, turning the giant press into an elephant, bringing in the jungle motif, which was also mostly in my head in the early drafts.

Another important change I made during the revision process was to focus on one time, one shift at work, as opposed to more of a summary approach. I cut words like *some days* and *would* and made all the verbs active and present tense to heighten the immediacy of the poem.

The first title I gave the poem, in draft three, was "Tarzan in the Factory." I had that comparison in the back of my mind from the beginning—the whole idea of swinging through the jungle is the iconic image of Tarzan—but it hadn't emerged on the page yet. One of the big issues for me concerned where to bring Tarzan into the poem. It took three more drafts before I discovered the final title, "Factory Jungle." That title established the central metaphoric landscape of the poem and allowed it to build up to mentioning Tarzan. The "Tarzan" title seemed to make the whole process too pat and to remove the sense of surprise from the poem. It simplified things into a joke, when I felt like I wanted to get at something much more serious. Another thing about working in a factory that was unlike Tarzan was that you were burdened with a lot of necessary safety gear; so when I imagined flying out of the factory on those ropes, I also imagined shedding all of that— "boots, coveralls, safety glasses, ear plugs." Tarzan, after all, was nearly naked, and that represents another kind of freedom.

As I continued working on the poem, I came upon the crucial realization—that Tarzan wouldn't have been able to be heard over the din of that factory. Even Tarzan, King of the Jungle, would be licked by *this* jungle, and that realization gave me my last line: "yelling louder than Tarzan ever had to." I initially wrote past that ending, bringing in Jane and Cheetah, but I was leaning on the joke too much. The important thing was the dream of escape, not so much what to escape to. (I certainly had no use for a monkey.) I tend to write past my endings, to explain too much, in early drafts. Early on, I'm

23

not sure where the poem is going, so I blow right past the true last line without even recognizing it.

Like all of my poems, this one went through many drafts before I thought it was good enough to earn an OK tag—although poetry has its own quality control inspectors called editors. But that's another story.

Loving the Flesh

How surprised we are to find we live here,
Here within our bodies.
—ERIC PANKEY

Last night I lay beside you, unable to sleep,
and read the stories written on my cells by one
who long ago breathed into dust, shaped flesh
from earth and deemed it good, who set me
in the boat of my mother's womb rocking.
How could I imagine a heaven without
these legs, these arms, this heart that beats
inside the cage of my chest, blood pumping
outward like the first days when sap rises
to meet the warmth of some late winter sun?

Tonight after dinner as we spoke to one another
in that careless, sleepy way we do when the children
have left us with nothing more than our love
and its weariness, you told me that the things
of this world were far too heavy for you to carry
into the next, that you hoped one day death
would be a move toward something better, like leaving
an old house with no more than a backward glance.

But what of the pear, I said, whose perfect skin shines
in the basket by the window, and what of Christ

25

who could not leave this earth without his love
for the woman who drew water from the well,
without first cooking fish for those he knew
could never hold fast: Cool breeze of morning
coming onto shore, bread warming hands
that still ached from holes not yet healed, fire
burnt down to a circle of coal and ash.

Now going up the stairs to our room I think
about how tomorrow morning the rabbit will leave
his den, how the early light will move against the far wall
and we will wake to each other's body, how you will allow
me to kiss the top of your head, line of scar near the corner
of your mouth, the narrow bone of your shoulder blade
that peeks out from under your gown, your breasts
that tip away from your chest, like our minds when we forget
that we would not know a soul if it were not draped by skin
and muscle, by tendon upon bone, by artery and vein entwined.

THE BODY OF POETRY

I couldn't ignore the role the body plays in the writing of poems, even if I
wished to. The very act of putting pen to paper or fingertips to keyboard (or
voice to tape for that matter) conjures up the physical body I reside in—or
more properly put—the body I *am*. There's no escaping it: my fingers hold a
pen or roll from key to key as I type; my throat constricts and relaxes as I say
the words over and over; I have no choice but to feel the way the tongue must
bend or extend toward the sounds that conjure images of some other
moment, some other bodily movement.

And it's not just my body that informs my work. As my wife Shelly re-
minds me, all too often it's her breasts, her bottom, her legs and arms and
neck, the curve of her face and lift of her nose, that are being transcribed. My
parents and sons, my grandparents and nieces and nephews, are all standing
there in the glory of their flesh as well, and it's the lyric that seems most ap-
propriate for these kinds of moments and revelations, these movements that
connect the body and poetry to each other—the way stone latches to stone in
their placement in a wall, the way soil clings to the seed until rain pushes life
outward from it.

The "appropriateness" to which I refer is inextricably tied (at least in my mind) to the corporeal nature of our existence. Who among us does not experience the world through the biology of our being? Each of our senses—if we've been blessed with these faculties fully functioning—ties us to this world and to our place in it, like the tethers of a balloon or a sailing ship, and while there may be some among us who wish they *could* sever such tethers, free themselves to float into the seemingly infinite sky or to drift upon the equally vast waters of some metaphysical sea, the reality remains that even if the ropes of certain senses come undone—cut by the knife of a cataclysmic experience or gently untied by long neglect—even in the darkness of this absence, the silence—the lack of taste or smell or touch—even in this place of want, we would not be removed absolutely from our bodies. There would still be the rhythms our hearts choose based upon our level of exertion or the emotions that sway us in a given moment; there would still be our lungs expanding to take in the air that staves off death, the food we must eat to fire our metabolic engine, the complex systems of digestion, and the most base (and perhaps miraculous) function of removing from our bodies what can no longer be of use. As Maxine Kumin says, "We eat, we evacuate, survivors that we are."

The lyric, at least in part, punctuates our act of *being*, of *surviving*. A successful lyric—with its undulating rhythm, the rise and fall of the hills it traverses, the tall grasses grown brown, the goldenrod still draping the field with its yellow scarves—depends upon the physical world. The lyric mirrors our breathing; it asks us to stop chasing after the hectic, worrisome ways of a culture bent on production at all cost; it asks us to enter the Western world's equivalent of Zen's insistence upon the present moment, or Emerson's *ever-present now* which, although it tries to suggest some sense of the infinite, is ultimately only attainable by our embeddedness in the specific moment, our sinking deeper into an exact physical space and time, fixed to the earth.

By emptying myself in order to see more fully the life before me, I encounter the sacred that Whitman saw in a blade of grass, that Issa recorded as wild geese passed the mountains of Shinano, that Shinkichi Takahashi opens for the reader when he contemplates the crow or rat. In these kinds of moments, I begin to become something other than I am. By imitating—via the modality of language—I am presented with the possibility of unlocking part of this thing that I am not, and in doing so, I privilege not myself but this thing that is other than the self. "Better to impersonate than to / Personify, when it comes to nature," James Galvin suggests, and how much richer our lives might be if we heeded this suggestion, if we began to focus on this movement away from self and deeper into another, if we attempted to impersonate a bobcat or a cardinal flower, if in this recognition of our own body and the bodies of others, we could imagine the ways all bodies intersect. Of course, this movement, which I place faith in, is ultimately a linguistic

27

maneuver because the self I cannot escape must use the language the self helps to create, and although I hope to step beyond my own scope of vision, in the end I cannot depart from my own body, my own material existence. Having said that, this is the best we can do, and while the wondrous phenomenon of language falls short again and again, it is a failure most writers would gladly embrace, and one which, at the very least, acknowledges the mystery of existence that lies beyond us.

        ∾

Maybe we're enamored with the lyric because it allows us to change everything, allows us to become, at least linguistically, something else. Northrop Frye suggests that the lyric is "an internal mimesis of sound and imagery"; in other words, in the act of imitation (mimesis) the poem takes on sounds and images of the lived thing, the bodily, fully infused fleshliness of the world. The alchemy of poetry is its ability to transmogrify the flesh: Look, it says, your hand is an indigo bunting flying over the slender river of your wife's back, and her love in return has trailed after you like the tracks of the bobcat following a flock of turkey toward the hemlocks that rise up along the streambed—and in all of this, that thing—the beloved and our yearning for the beloved, in some ways a search more mystical than rational—becomes something else, something closer to the ineffable thing it is, in the bonds of metaphor.

Words, too, become something else, and that something else winds its way around the flesh. The electricity of connection (a phrase that is surely not metaphor when one considers the physiology of the brain) literally triggers our synapses as we digest words from the printed page. Such physical interaction must take place if we are to first read, then make meaning, next interpret, and finally to change the self—at times in profound ways and at other times in ways so subtle they are imperceptible to others and even to ourselves.

Another way to look at what we might call the metallurgical quality of language within the lyrical tradition is to examine the legacy or mark it leaves on others. These scratchings on parchment, these grunts and groans as we speak, ripple outward touching the flesh of others, writing upon the very cells that compose them and comprise their lives, possibly altering them, shifting the direction their feet might take, the manner in which they might strike or caress the skin of another. Every poem written, every poem read requires some kind of response from a human being: a nonplussed sigh, an ecstatic groan, a brotherly amen.

        ∾

Stanley Kunitz suggests that the "most poignant of all lyric tensions stems from the awareness that we are living and dying at once." Following a similar thread, in my poem "Prairie Liturgy" I claim that "only upon our failing breath may we speak." The act of speaking a poem into existence—Can a poem exist in its fullest sense if it remains unspoken?—may only occur as we exhale, as the most vital element of life leaves our body. When we speak, in one sense we give the very breath of our life to another, but if we are to survive, we must stop speaking so that we may once again draw the breath of life back into our lungs. In these physical transactions we are silenced by our own body's needs, given time in which to think, to compose, to prepare, and then to continue with the making of the poem which is winding its way out of our lives. In those moments in which we do not speak, let us pray that we learn to listen as the person in whose presence we stand offers a portion of his or her life to us in return. Maybe the best way to think about inhalation is as an act of reflection, of absorbing the rhythms of speech that have shaken our flesh, and exhalation as the creation that comes out of such reflection.

∽

The title of Czeslaw Milosz's *Unattainable Earth* suggests the paradox of the lyric: that while it is the earth we wish to attain, that we make attempt after attempt to realize in the act of making the poem, it is the earth that remains unattainable, unachievable. It is the body that I love, that I adore—the earth's and my own and my wife's and my sons' and so on. It is the body that mesmerizes with the miracle of its creation, its intricacies, its secrets whispered through the tunnels of veins and arteries, its language spoken so clearly in the flex of muscle and tendon. Yet it is the body that ultimately must fail: mortality in partnership with the miraculous. And it is in this way that I look at the lyric, marvel at it and mourn it and embrace it again and again. Yes, the lyric offers the possibilities of the miraculous—somehow capturing, if only momentarily, some part of the world's body—but the lyric also is always doomed to fail (if we see failure as the inability to transcend mortality.) Perhaps it is better to see the finite nature of the lyric not as a limitation, but like the body, as an integral part of its composition, something that will allow other life to grow from it.

∽

In *A Poetry Handbook*, Mary Oliver describes the lyric poem as one "likely to employ a simple and natural rather than an intricate or composed musicality." Such a statement returns me to the body and its relationship to the poem. The shapes and sizes we take on over the course of our lives, although controlled in part by the genes we inherit, do not tell the final story of our bodies. In this day and age, our obsessions with diets and plastic surgery and body sculpting through weight training and cardio workouts betray us as a nation of formalists, superimposing a composed musicality of six-pack abs and hour-glass figures, a preordained form into which we hope to pour our bodily existence. Similarly, many of us shape our lawns through the artifice of landscaping and chemical treatments, introducing nonnative species, watering and mowing and watering and mowing. While all poetry must concede a degree of artifice, I find it far better to be like the gardener who embraces native plants and trees, who arranges her landscaping in a manner that suggests how life might flourish without our formal intervention, sustaining itself in an intricate relationship with what grows around it.

It is my hope that the writer of the lyrical poem will study the native language of a given situation, the indigenous rhythms that must be present in the poem if a degree of authenticity is to be achieved. The physical details of what is being impersonated in the poem—which in turn unlocks the emotional details—seldom are sacrificed to structures and rules beyond its own scope. Instead the writer of such a poem takes the loam from the streambed that winds its way through the subject, and like a potter, she learns the different qualities of this clay, works it on the wheel until she begins to discover the shape it wishes to take. This is the discourse—perhaps the word *commerce* is even closer to the idea—between the body and the poem that comprises the lyric impulse.

How does the clay shape us, and how do we shape the clay? How does its physical existence define our own corporeal way of life and vice versa? I hope we never definitively answer this question because it's in the mystery of the pull and tug, the coupling of the body and language, the body and experience, that I hope to spend my days touching and molding the poem, firing it in the kiln of our existence and in the writing that helps us to understand it.

Chris Dombrowski

Elegy with Fall's Last Filaments

In the one world
you called twin
tired of being
misidentified how
swiftly you became
the spider mending
each day its
wind-rent web and not
the box-elder beetle you
had been grasshopper
still tearing
at the ties intricate void
bright bardo room
she I call her hangs
like a home light
beneath the eaves and you
would have left her on

All kinds of kindnesses
Luka just two
at noon yesterday
where'd the moon go
daddy The neighbors'
plums landing ripely

in our lawn Portrait
of you as webstrand
stretched between
the fences   Sky-
deep lake appearing
halfway into my hike
as if it knew I were
thirsty—sat down
sketched the swale
in one broad stroke
fainter lines for where
the fog had hung
and almost asked
if you'd found
a formlessness yet
didn't—tempting
to pick a few
forget-me-knots
marking the soundless
rill

Stir a little
shallows with your
alderleaf archipelagos
branch and cloud
reflections drawn
so crisply I mistake
one white trunk for
the other   Stir
a little sawdust
from the just cut
deadfall firewood
tepeed now above
the tinder I light
before shucking

my shirt and jeans—
things *little soul little*
stray you used to make
fun of these the last
words you quoted me
asking *now where*
will you stay?
—and plunging
through the cold lake
body strung with quick-
silver sunlight leaking down
to fill escaping orbs
of air gone as you are
probably no one
joins anyone here or after
you said but perhaps
the silence we've
always expected from
the dead isn't
exactly silence

On surfacing
you want to have
something warm
to sit by tidy
fire tsk-tsking
this entire notion
but easing away
the gooseflesh
the body's automatic
response

On the hike out
plucked from a steaming
pile of blackbear scat

a huckleberry still whole
skin unblemished
large pupil in the
vitreous of my palm
who's watching
mote-midges blurring
through fruitless stems
unadorned lady-
bugs imago mayflies
the illustrious bound for webs
orbiting each other fall's
last filaments
kept thinking
law versus spirit
what we're told
versus what we're
told—no one no
spring to rinse
the fruit only
a watering mouth

ON "ELEGY WITH FALL'S LAST FILAMENTS"

Like many writers, I find it cumbersome to write about my own writing. I once heard Richard Ford say that talking about one's own work was like serving the feast that starves the masses. That shrewd notion complicates the conversation a bit, as does the fact that the poem in discussion, "Elegy with Fall's Last Filaments," arrived in a manner to which I was, and still am, unaccustomed.

The impetus of this poem was ultimately the passing away of a beloved friend and teacher, Patricia Goedicke, a poet whose own work dealt deftly with the form in question. *How does one write an elegy for a master of the elegiac mode?* was not a question that I consciously pondered during composition, but it must have been wagging its knobby finger in my brainstem and amygdala. The title, of course, riffs on Larry Levis's titles, such as "Elegy with a Thief in the Rigging" and "Elegy with a Thimbleful of Water in Its Cage" from his masterpiece *Elegy*. Also, a directive of sorts stemmed from his elegy-

34

turned-love poem "Garcia Lorca: A Photograph of the Granada Cemetery, 1966" from *Dollmaker's Ghost*, in which Levis writes of Lorca: "He would not want, tonight, another elegy." That line, and W. S. Merwin's famous "Who would I show it to" from "Elegy," weighed on me, and I think that while elegiac, "Elegy with Fall's Last Filaments" also questions the notion of elegy.

In late April 2006, I visited Patricia Goedicke in a Missoula hospital and witnessed a woman, aged seventy-five, whose body had been whittled down by countless bouts with cancer but whose mind and spirit thrived. I marveled at her vitality: between chemo treatments, she revised poems, read Dante, shook her fist at politicians in the news. We talked of where to find the season's first morels, of the afternoon light which took the color of the good glass of chardonnay she craved, of grocery store tulips—and then she grew almost instantly serious, intent on sharing a poem with me. "Little soul little stray," she recited, quoting Merwin's version of Hadrian's deathbed poem, "little drifter / now where will you stay / all pale and all alone / after the way / you used to make fun of things." Silly me, sane me, I thought it was the treatments talking; but it was something she wanted me to have, the last of many gifts, something she thought might help. After clawing against various forms of cancer for over two decades, she left the body on July 4, 2006.

"One loves only form," Charles Olson wrote, "and form only comes into existence when a thing is born"; a rigorous line, especially if we hope our poetic forms will become "merely an extension of content." Finding the right form, or being found by it, is to my mind one of the sweet rewards in poetry. "Form is the woods," Jim Harrison writes; conflate this with Robert Frost's rather prickly "Anyone can find his way into a poem, but only a poet can find his way out," and the inspired poet is placed appropriately deep within the forest attempting to deliver poem, reader, and speaker out of the trees in a meaningful, believable way. With its relatively skinny, punctuation-free lines, "Elegy with Fall's Last Filaments" was formally a surprise, quite different territory from the poems I had been working on. As I approached the poem, or the poem approached me, I heard a syntax that I sensed enacted the disequilibrium I felt. As they took shape, the odd little linear units of sound and meaning, which formally resembled, curiously, "Little Soul," began to allow for a tentative, testing voice that attempted to embrace the fleeting.

But how "thinky" all that sounds! Perhaps a more authentic description of the poem's genesis would go like this: There was a big garden spider in its seemingly indestructible web above our porch, and Patricia's line, "Death be my homelight," which I read at her memorial in late September after failing to process her loss for months; a crude sketch of a cold lake into which I dived, and the lake itself, cold enough to recall Kierkegaard's "only he who descends into the netherworld rescues the beloved"; the sense that the fragile withered beloved had become part of the irreproachable ineffable, and the strange feeling of simultaneously extending a conversation and taking dictation (very strange and hard to say); a fuguelike flash that lasted an hour or so each evening for several days, accompanied by Bach's *Suites for Unaccompanied Cello* and the ever-long October light.

Dan Gerber

To W. S. Merwin

I was struck this morning,
reading your ode, "To the Blank Spaces,"
how it reminded me of your recent letter
I have been in the process of trans-
scribing from your cryptic hand,
typing it out, but for the words
I have yet to decipher from context—
how the gaps fill in, with patience,
the way proud flesh bridges a cut
or a small equation seems to solve itself
in the mind-space of turning
to the quotidian, how
the pond water, for example,
resettles itself to the image of this duck,
fresh from who knows where.

TRANSLATING MY WAY INTO A POEM

It isn't every day that the world arranges itself in a poem.
—WALLACE STEVENS

I was having a wonderful correspondence with W. S. Merwin, exchanging handwritten letters composed, as he put it, "not on a gadget," which I also greatly prefer, although Merwin's hand can, at times, be difficult to decipher.

Sometimes it would take long hours to get the gist of a letter and then another day to discern all the fine points that I worked on as one might a translation, or, it occurs to me, a revision of one's own poem, the first draft of which had been put aside long enough to begin to forget and then come back to with at least a little more perspective than had been available in that first mysterious moment of taking it down.

My method was to type out the letter as best I could, leaving blank spaces for the words, or in some cases, phrases, not yet translated, and then to read it over to see what occurred to me from context. One of the words I struggled with turned out to be *iconostasis*, the difficulty with which I think I can be forgiven. Often, when I'd studied a mystifying configuration of letters in relation to the known words on either side of it, my eyes would water and begin to cross; I'd have to put away both letter and typescript. And I found that when I came back to it a day or so later, after having turned my attention elsewhere, the recalcitrant word would reveal itself so clearly and obviously I'd marvel that it could have ever seemed so obscure.

While I was so engaged with one of Merwin's letters, I also happened to be reading his collection of odes *Present Company,* and, more particularly, the one called "To the Blank Spaces," in which the poet sees beyond the words of his own poem into the pattern of the spaces separating and encompassing them until he sees the spaces finally, not as simply a random series of gaps, but rather as "all words out of one language," and finally as "tracks of the same creature."

As a poet, or any artist, learns to trust and to give him- or herself up to the process by which the work reveals itself, he begins to see that what may have seemed only a random series of images in the moment of creation bear a definite and incontrovertible relationship that, once discovered, can no longer go unnoticed! And it was at just such a moment that I began to take down, almost as though from dictation, my own poem "To W. S. Merwin." I wrote it in one sitting and the next day, coming back to it, I made one slight edit. So finally, it seems, I owe this poem to W. S. Merwin, to his poem "To the Blank Spaces," and to the cryptic hand of his wonder-filled letters.

Jeff Gundy

Contemplation with Ledges and Moon

What do the hollows in the stone promise?
Where the scratched names stop, the rock mutters

what it meant all along. Here, the grizzled red maple.
There, yellow beech clenched hard to the cliff side,

a tulip tree smooth forty feet up. Edges blur
in the half-light, and the swallows work higher

and higher, and the bats revel, stretching
their thin webs around what they need.

The mind is a rattly gourd, the ego, a black marble.
The soul is very light and large, a cloud of leaves

that froth and fade into the wood thrush's cry.
There is no soul without the shy veery,

the whiny bugs hunting our heat, the gravel
working its way out from sandstone.

The soul is not a language or a cat or a catapult.
It is a net without mesh, a sail knuckling and filling

39

among fireflies and gauzy leaves, flowing into
every valley, filling every breath and stone, spinning,

keening, rising, dusty heartwood, silken fog.
The broken path through trees made us stumble,

but we found the wide meadow at last
where the great golden moon lifted up

from the well of her sleep and sent down
more borrowed light than we needed

as we cried out and whispered on our way.

WRITING INTO THE EVENING

When my friend and fellow poet Terry Hermsen first took me along on one
of his "poetry night hikes," I was skeptical. I had almost always written alone,
and the idea of being herded around and then told to write on command
smacked of group-think and guided tours. But I went along and found some-
thing close to magical in the process. I have done it half a dozen times now,
as participant and leader, and it's simple enough, never quite the same twice,
but not hard to replicate.

In brief, all that's needed is to gather a willing group, set out as the light
fades, wander for as long as you have through more or less natural terrain, and
try to keep the chatter to a minimum. Stop here and there to look at the
landscape and read some poems or lyrical prose aloud, just to hear some beau-
tiful language. (I can still hear Terry reciting Robert Bly's "Surprised by
Evening" and Pattiann Rogers's "Suppose Your Father Is a Redbird.") Just as
it starts to get really dark, settle in somewhere (a waterfall or stream is nice, as
is a sunset, but nothing is mandatory). Read or recite a little more; then get
out the pens and notebooks and write whatever comes until you can't see to
write any more.

On this particular occasion we wandered through the Nelson Ledges in
Cuyahoga Valley National Park, where fifteen or twenty of us were taking
part in a weeklong nature writing institute, and ended up at a nearby over-
look. In the beautiful dusk the rocks and trees seemed luminous as we walked
slowly among them. I had been reading obscure and speculative treatises on

the nature of the soul for some time, and some of these ideas came back as I settled in among the others on my rocky seat and pulled out my notebook. These ideas were interwoven with what I had seen as we walked and the inevitable summer mosquitoes.

As I started writing, with the evening coming on around us and all the things of the natural world going about their business, I began to feel that I was simply another part of the world about my own work—not some alienated, distanced observer—but a full member of the universe, different in details but not in kind from the bats, the trees, and the rocks. And so in the middle part of the poem I began to circle more widely around and away from the immediate impressions of the place, spinning out one metaphor after another for the soul, careless of logic and consistency, suddenly confident that whatever I wrote would hold together somehow.

Soon, it grew too dark to write (although some of us kept going even when we were scrawling by feel alone), and we had to head home. I was pleased with what I'd written, as much as I could remember, although I was not sure what it would look like when I came back to it, and even less sure that I had found an ending. Fortunately for the poem, the experience was not quite over. The last eight lines describe more or less directly the passage back to the cars: we walked a tricky, root-laden stretch through trees and then came out into a broad meadow with the brilliant moon above. That silent opening was so sudden and glorious that the whole group seemed to shudder; for a few moments, it seemed to me, and I think to everyone, as though we were truly at home in the universe, that something much bigger and wilder than we was offering its blessing.

The first chance I got, I sat down again—with a good light this time—and tried to fit that last part of the evening into words that might do it justice without tipping over entirely into sentiment. Then I took a clean sheet of paper and began the exacting, exhilarating work of making all my messy notes into a poem.

The poem has gone through several revisions, first longhand and then on my computer, though its main contours have not changed much. For the last few years I have been writing a lot of poems in two- or three-line stanzas with longish lines, and this poem fell rather quickly into that pattern. While revising, I tried to weed out or strengthen any weak and sloppy phrasings, cut what seemed to be redundant or irrelevant passages, and think hard about rhythm and lineation and pacing, although lacking very precise language for them.

I tried, as I often do, to walk that fine line between the sublime and the ridiculous, weaving what I know are bold and large claims about the nature of things with particulars of the landscape and the moment, trying not to slip into ponderous abstraction or heavy insistence that those claims are the truth. I tried to make something that would be, first of all, a beautiful shape made of words, an artifact in language whose patterns of sound and imagery not only describe an event and reflect upon it but become a new experience when spoken aloud or read on the page.

Kimiko Hahn

Pink

From testing on thirteen dead piglets
buried six months in a Scottish bog

then exhumed to note *levels of preservation*—

one exploded on touch, a second, reduced to fragments—
there's a lesson on *limited exposure*:

the lover who ruled against love two nights in a row
or another who couldn't abide slinky blouses.

I, too, preserve varying degrees of loss at high cost.
Pink linoleum. Pink fishnets. Pink piglet

at the county fair that decomposing summer.

The Ferris wheel in the pink twilight
and going off on a tear

with the town coroner who sought rapture in casual rupture.

On "Pink"

By studying the remains of piglets buried in bogs, Ms. Gill-Robinson . . . also determined that limited exposure to air and shorter burial times were also significant in assuring preservation. . . . Each of the three peat bogs in the experiment contained different environments, resulting in various levels of preservation. One piglet, buried for 17 months, exploded upon gentle touch. . . . Other piglets were reduced to fragments of muscular and skeletal remains.
—From the *Science Times* article by Anahad S. O'Connor,
"Piglets Buried in Bogs a Clue to Mystery"

Inspired by this article, I wrote then published a poem several years ago. At the time the version looked right—but in hindsight, it didn't feel quite right. And I should have gone with that feeling, after all. *After all* should be the test. But I'd placed the poem inside a poetic-diary (Japanese-style) and the composition seemed to address my hesitation. Again, emphasis on *seemed*.

Pink

From a report on fourteen dead piglets
buried six months in a Scottish bog

then exhumed to note stages of preservation—

one exploded upon touch, a second, reduced to fragments—

there's a lesson on limited exposure.

That is, the lover who ruled against love two nights in a row

or another who couldn't take slinky fabric.

I, too, preserve varying degrees of loss at high cost.
Pink linoleum. Pink fishnets. Pink piglet

at the county fair that decomposing summer.

Fear of the pink ferris wheel, that same twilight
and of showing it—

to those who seek rapture in casual rupture.

With new editorial distance, I looked to see where the poem radiated,
pulsed. *Limited exposure? Explode?* The closure felt off. Add another line?

. . .

I, too, preserve varying degrees of loss at high cost.
Pink linoleum. Pink fishnets. Pink piglet

at the county fair that decomposing summer.

Fear of the pink ferris wheel, that same twilight
and of showing it—

to those who seek rapture in casual rupture.
Going off on a tear—?

I tried a different closure by switching the *loss* line:

. . . slinky fabric.
Pink linoleum. Pink fishnets. Pink piglet

at the county fair that decomposing summer.

Fear of the pink ferris wheel, that same twilight
and of showing it—

to those who seek rapture in casual rupture.
I, too, preserve varying degrees of loss at high cost.

I tried ending on *pink* for both the cute and vulgar:

Pink piglet. . .
Pink lights and linoleum. Pink fishnets everywhere.

45

I added more to the "pink" list:

> . . . slinky fabric.

> I, too, preserve varying degrees of loss at high cost.
> From the pink piglet at the county fair

> to the pink ferris wheel that decomposing summer
> and in its twilight, of going off on a tear

> with those who seek rapture in casual rupture—

But something was still missing. On a train trip I opened to the piece again. I had to admit that the ending didn't allow for real resonance. There wasn't enough room for feelings. Once I admitted that, I had to move back to my earlier question.

Over and over I had circled "stages of preservation" and "limited exposure." I looked at these two "moments" and reconsidered what I had thought the poem was about. I wondered if I had gotten stuck on the phrase, "a lesson on limited exposure," and that because it is phrased as "a lesson," the idea overwhelmed "preservation." Something had to give but I wasn't ready to give up "preserving loss" which was more interesting than, say, "chance exposure"—which I tried inserting. So I played with *lesson*. I returned to the original article to see if I could lift other phrases and came up with "clues to mysteries." A mouthful and *clues* maybe not necessary. Good questions.

I still missed a sense of the poem breaking open somewhere—a *rupture*. I looked at the last line for an opportunity and tried the word *those*:

> I, too, preserve loss [at high cost]:
> from catching the pink piglet at the county fair

> to swinging atop the pink ferris wheel
> that decomposing summer

> and in its twilight, going off on a tear
> with ????? who seek rapture in casual rupture—

Something specific and/or personal. I scribbled in the margin: "one, man." Then decided to give the man an occupation:

professor [cliché]
farm hand [not specific enough?]
janitor [reminds me of grade school]
entomologist [closer]
biologist [too general]

I liked the scientist who could be local and weird (and echoed the bog re-search), but I also wanted an image that would go with the county fair, some-thing potentially seedy and suggesting the speaker's recklessness.

carnie [too obvious]
4-H leader [mouthful and too weird—draws too much attention]
trucker [cliché]
pilot [generalish]
medic [general]
engineer [ditto]
DJ [reminds me of Bee Gees]
medical examiner [closer]
anthropologist [general]
geologist [still general]

I liked "medical examiner" but it was a mouthful. "Coroner"? Not seedy, per se. "Local coroner"?

I also reconsidered some of the one- and two-line stanzas that have become a stylistic preference—to draw attention to diction. I changed *reports* to *experiments* then to *testing* for the sake of cadence. Stayed with the title (which was once "Limited Exposure") because of the vulgar connotation. Put *pink* back into the twilight image now that the line was further from the first two. I looked at end/near-end words again to tease out more slant. Changed *local* to town for the cadence although I prefer the word and connotation of *local*.

Pink

From testing on thirteen dead pigs
buried six months in a Scottish bog

then exhumed to note levels of preservation—

one exploded when touched, another was reduced to fragments—
there's a lesson on the mysterious.

A lover rules against love two nights in a row
while a boyfriend can't abide slinky blouses.

I, too, preserve loss at high cost:
from catching the pink piglet at the county fair

to swinging atop the pink ferris wheel
that decomposing summer

and, in its pink twilight, going off on a tear

with a local coroner who sought rapture in casual rupture—

Then, about a week later, I felt that "limited exposure" was more interest-
ing than "preservation" and tried adding it as the last words.

. . .

with a town coroner who sought rapture in casual rupture.
Or what a scientist might call, *limited exposure.*

Another several weeks later, I returned to the version that was published
three years ago: I saw that I had scraped out a line that felt essential again. I
replaced it as well as "limited exposure." Not surprisingly, this next version is
somewhere in between that earlier one and these later ones. I'm still reconsid-
ering "fear."

Pink

From testing on thirteen dead pigs
buried six months in a Scottish bog

then exhumed to note *levels of preservation*—

one exploded on touch, a second, reduced to fragments—
there's a lesson on *limited exposure*:

the lover who ruled against love two nights in a row
or another who couldn't abide slinky blouses.

I, too, preserve varying degrees of loss at high cost.
Pink linoleum. Pink fishnets. Pink piglet

at the county fair that decomposing summer.

Fear of the Ferris wheel in that pink twilight
and going off on a tear

with the town coroner who sought rapture in casual rupture.

Finally, from writing this essay I realize that, not only does my intuitive
process include dynamics (dialectical opposites such as *bury/expose*), but also
the desire for a qualitative leap: where the poem leaps from being a bunch of
words to being an experience. An experience for me and, I hope, for the
reader. This is the reason I continue testing it for a sense of *rupture*.

William Heyen

Longhouse

A seventeen-year-old Onondaga County boy admitted that he
    & a younger friend

had been drinking, had jumped a fence at the village pond
    to attack a Mute Swan,

Obie, who met them to defend his nesting mate.
    The boys killed him,

left his head on steps at the entrance of the police station.
    In court,

they confessed they'd tortured & stabbed Obie repeatedly,
    then broken his legs. . . .

The Swan's head lay at the station's entrance
    for several hours

before discovery that morning. During those hours, Obie's eyes,
    open or closed,

absorbed the last signals of starlight, & whatever birdcalls
    tinged their cells,

as dawn awakened this village once part of the Iroquois longhouse
where two of our teenagers

climbed a fence to torture & decapitate a winged creature, then
left its head here.

FROM THE OUT-THERE

A few times a year I'll tear a story out of a newspaper or magazine. I tear it out rather than scissor it neatly because I want a feeling of unplanned offhandedness, not one of careful consideration. And I save a particular story not because of its Googleable facts or empirical information but because something in it has connected with me in a way I can't quite articulate—something residing in my deepest mind, something from childhood or the womb, something.

I don't remember how long I had the clipping with me before my poem "Long-house" showed up, but probably several years. (Obits on the back of this clipping tell me that these events took place in 1994. My poem appeared in a magazine in 2000, and in my book *The Rope* in 2004.) Sometimes a poem directly or indirectly generated by the topical will appear in my notebook hours later, sometimes years (and sometimes there are many drafts, of course). I usually read the news story many times, allowing it to write itself in me, if it will. I try not to understand it, but to fathom it, sound it. Above all, I do not want to force it.

Many aspects of this brief report still intrigue me: the *Star Wars* name given to the male mute swan; how it rose to the defense of its mate; the story's location in the land of one of the tribes of the Iroquois; the sadistic nature of the crime; the ages of the perpetrators; the community's loathing. But I know that what hit me hardest was that after the

Community furious over swan's slaying

MANLIUS — A community's loathing has shocked the father of a teen-ager accused of stabbing and beheading a swan at a village park. Daniel Doney has received threatening letters and telephone calls since he has been publicly identified and no longer goes to Fayetteville-Manlius High School in Onondaga County because it would be "too dangerous" for him.

Murderers are not treated as viciously, said Floyd Doney, Daniel's father. On Thursday night, nearly 100 people showed up for Daniel Doney's arraignment in Manlius Village Court. The majority were angered by the mindless slaying of the swan on April 30.

Doney, 17, of DeWitt, Onondaga County, pleaded innocent to criminal mischief, criminal trespass and cruelty to animals.

Doney and a 15-year-old admitted they had been drinking on the day the swan was slain. Police said the teens jumped the fence at the Manlius Swan Pond April 30 and attacked Obie, a mute male swan, as it came to the defense of its nesting mate. The creature's head was left at the entrance to the Manlius Police Station.

Authorities have withheld the name of the other boy, sentenced Friday by a Family Court judge to 1,000 hours of community service after admitting he tortured and stabbed Obie repeatedly, then broke his legs.

Judge Bryan Hedges also ordered the youth to pay $300 for his half of the cost of the dead boys mutilated Obie—swan of my childhood, swan of Yeats's "Leda and the Swan" and "The Wild Swans at Coole," swan of Budd Schulberg's book *Swan Watch*, black swan of Düsseldorf I photographed decades ago, emotional echo of every swan I have ever seen—they left his head at the entrance to the police station. No doubt everything in me of disgust, anger, impatience, and dread regarding aberrant behavior was evoked by their criminal act. I was far from a perfect teenager myself, got drunk and into trouble in sometimes imaginative and embarrassing ways, and was lucky that I eventually wised up; yet there was never anything in me that "tortured and stabbed . . . repeatedly, then broke . . . legs," never anything in me that so brazenly and unconsciously challenged and attempted to desecrate the community's moral and civil laws.

But a poem won't survive being declaimed from a morally superior pulpit, no matter its ostensible subject. "Longhouse" became a poem, it seems to me, when suddenly during the writing I threw myself behind the eyes of that head still receiving starlight and the tinges of birdcalls as dawn awakens the village where a sacred relationship once existed between creatures and human inhabitants. The long concluding sentence beginning "During those hours" came to me without forethought. I—the I that I am within the poem—seem not to want to let the swan be dead, seem to want to keep it within the processes of a universal life. In any case, my poem is quiet, controlled, understated, but at the same time may be on the verge of a radical and responsible anger—after all, these are *our* teenagers. And what they did is now left *here*, in the poem, in our place, imposed on us, on beauty, on order, on communal memory itself.

In short, then, a story from the out-there might by way of deepest unconscious pressures in us generate a rhythm, a sound, a duration of empathy and imagination in us, a poem.

awash with blushing textures, your hips, lipped lilies,

sex as song. I feel lost here
with just sequence to correct
my view. Against so much glass
starlight shuts a harsh door. This
is my tentative guitar,
communicating by touch
the passage to the river,
wanting above all to feel,
obliquely on your body,
the light. The airs I sing all
long for feathers. **There is no
avoiding** oblivion,
even for embodied gods,
horses grazing side by side.

The hand that anticipated everything—

There Is No Avoiding

Process may offer discovery. A person throwing the I Ching seeks the vatic in patterns from apparently random manipulation of counters—yarrow stalks or pennies—and though I don't posit the work of a personified agent—the hand of chance, the hand of God—to fill with meaning the processes in which I participate to write my poems, I do expect to be rewarded with discovery when I trust the language, which though it be no person does have agency enough to tender revelation to anyone willing to attend. Process for me is one mode of attention, a way of plowing the ground of language, unearthing coins (coigns) and ordnance (ordonnance) and bones (boons) buried generations back.

Awash as we are in scandal and suasion (which celebrity has cellulite, which beer brings more babes), small wonder we assume a lyric poem ought to gossip, sell you *my* feelings as yours, fondle anecdote, dotingly display another knick-knack in the curio cabinet. I don't doubt that poems may start with feeling and apply language to it, but the poems I myself want to write start with language and seek feeling there, are less Wordsworthian than Wittgensteinian: not emotion recollected in tranquility, but a bumping of one's head against the limits of language.

"There is no avoiding" began, then, not in my feelings but in someone else's words. This poem is part of a 34-poem sequence entitled "All the One-Eyed Boys in Town," itself part of a book, *Legible Heavens*, published in 2008 by Etruscan Press. Some features of the sequence may be seen in the poem, such as circularity: each poem begins where the last left off, usually in the middle of a sentence, and ends, usually in the middle of another sentence, where the next begins; a pattern that includes the last poem's ending in the middle of a sentence that the first poem finishes, so that in principle any of the poems might serve for a starting point. The title (identified in bold) lives within the poem, rather than standing outside and above it. Together the titles themselves make a poem that appears in the book's table of contents. Formally, the individual poems follow a simple syllabic pattern: 12-syllable first line, fourteen 7-syllable lines, 12-syllable last line.

More often than not, I write poems in/as sequences. I marvel at the fractality of language, its manumission of meaning at any level—phoneme (mmmmm!), word (damn!), phrase (of course), clause, sentence, line, paragraph, work, oeuvre—so I work hard *not* to assume that a poem is the fundamental unit, whole and isolated. I try not to take for granted, in other words, that a poetry book ought to be a "collection" of poems. Within a poem, we expect any given word to have its connotations curved by other words in the poem (the nun-ness of *wimpling* in "The Windhover" contrasts with *dauphin* and *chevalier*, its black-and-whiteness with *gold-vermilion*), but that also happens across poems (that the falcon wimples his wing "in his riding / Of the rolling level underneath him steady air" fathers-forth the "coiféd sisterhood" from which came "the tall nun" whose call "To the men in the tops and the tackle rode over the storm's brawling"). I assume that any of my poems ought to be modified by others, that my poetry ought to pursue arcs of meaning at all scales: within a line, and across books. Yes, I am building lines with words, and a poem with lines, but I am also building a sequence with poems. "All the One-Eyed Boys in Town" signals its focus on sequence even in its epigraph, through which Bruno Latour's *Iconoclash* warns that "the whole series has meaning, but none of its elements has any sense."

The process of this sequence began, as often my poetry does, with collection. I assembled a set of recent poetic sequences written by others (constru-

56

ing "poetic sequences" liberally enough to include a few works that call themselves fiction). The list on the book's acknowledgments page begins: John Ashbery, *Shadow Train*; Anne Carson, *The Beauty of the Husband*; Debra Di Blasi, *Drought*; Rachel Blau DuPlessis, *Drafts 1-38: Toll*; Carol Frost, *Abstractions*; Forrest Gander, *Torn Awake*. . . . From each listed work I collected phrases that engaged me; so in "There is no avoiding," which originates in phrases from C. D. Wright's *Deepstep Come Shining*, my notes begin like this:

C. D. Wright: *Deepstep Come Shining*

3: the ruby progression of taillights
4: it is unlike night
7: they would have been blue the eyes
8: ~~beautiful things~~ fill every vacancy
9: cold eyes are bad ~~to~~ eat
10: ~~there is no avoiding oblivion~~
13: ~~to correct the view~~
15: wonder who lives there
16: Get your bearings. Hear the trees.
21: crudely executed
22: ~~except for sex and song~~
23: take a mirror ~~to the river~~
25: never never never
27: this land became known as
28: I've been shouldering one rock at a time
29: of tenderness in the world
31: that they have a treeless afterlife
32: the fingers limber and lengthen
33: the sweating silver vase with sunflowers

And so on through that book's one hundred plus pages.

Next I pieced portions of the collected text into a draft poem. Strikethroughs in the notes indicate passages used in the draft. By rule every word of the draft had to occur in the source text, so even a ligature like *to* in the draft came from a passage, here the passage from page 9. Once all thirty-four drafts were done, revisions began. I applied various rules, such as insisting that the word *sequence* had to be inserted in place of some two-syllable word in each poem. I went through multiple rounds of word-shifting: removing a word from one poem, inserting it in place of a word with the same syllable count in the next poem, inserting the newly displaced word into the following poem, and so on. By the time the sequence was finished, a few phrases remained intact (e.g. "there is no avoiding oblivion" here), but most had been modified (e.g., "beautiful things" became "embodied gods"). If the work succeeds (that big if from which a poet never can be free), even unaltered phrases are made new by dislocation and relocation.

The process(es) behind this poem and the sequence in which it is enrolled may appear to diminish the role of my subjectivity. To some, the processes will look dependent ("Those aren't even *your* words!") and mechanical ("You're not *writing*, you're just playing games!"). Such objections, though, seem to me to beg the question, to take for granted the anecdotality of the lyric. Against the objection of dependency, I note only that *all* language is received and manipulated, and I appeal to Harold Bloom's lovely apothegm, "The meaning of a poem can only be another poem." Against the objection that my processes are mechanical, I assert that even such apparently arbitrary rules as word shifting *in*clude my subjectivity rather than *ex*clude it. I must choose the word in each case. (And I select or make up each rule.) The application of rules, I contend, creates multiple occasions for the assertion of my subjectivity.

I don't presume to recollect emotion in tranquility, as if my emotion had been collected once, and now came trailing clouds of glory. I don't presume to express my feelings, as if I knew before the poem what my feelings are. I am not sending a gift by means of language, as one sends a box by FedEx. I assume instead that the *language* knows more than I do, that if I will treat it, in Kantian fashion, also as an end and not merely as a means, it will reveal matters of consequence I might not otherwise know or feel or experience. I want in this way also to show respect to my poem's readers. My using the medium we share, the language, to report my experience or my internal state seems to me at high risk for condescension and narcissism. What reason have I to expect anyone else to care about or be edified by my feelings and thoughts? If, on the other hand, I find in the medium we share a means of discovery, *my* gaining from the shared medium some new perspective on my own experience seems to warrant hope that some similar new perspective might be available to others through the poem.

Or so I tell myself, to rationalize having done what there is no avoiding my doing.

John Hoppenthaler

Dance

Kirby Studio, MacDowell Colony, 2006

Eleven moths have attached themselves
to a weathered screen enclosing the porch.

Like some overzealous bouncer, it's blocked
their flight toward eternal attraction, floodlight

above the studio door. Something insistent
& genetic draws them toward the bulb, heat

& exposure, bids them begin again the frenzied
celebration of time that's left in summer flutter.

Doing so, might they nearly forget what
came before, earthbound crawl & pulse,

laborious spinning, the fitful sleep—
sisters, brothers snatched by hungry

birds on branches? I'm sorry to say this disco's
closed to the public for a private party,

lone mosquito & his long-legged date.
How easily they shift from waltz to tango;

59

how pleased they seem for the blazing spot-
light, rapt audience, the glow of romance

in ephemeral life. But a brazen gate-crasher
buzzes my ear; she whispers: *shut up & dance.*

Peterborough, NH, June 2006

Shut Up & Dance

I. Philandering

I tend to prefer poetry of the quotidian, which good poets show us is not so ordinary at all. In prose, Gabriel Garcia Marquez understands this; it's the *raison d'etre* for magical realism, framing the extraordinary ordinary. Poets are frequently stolidly wedded to their landscapes; that is to say, we write what we know. The danger of such monogamy is that life often grows common and ex-pected, so marked by rote activity that it deadens the soul, artistic vision. We fail to see the miraculous happening right in front of our eyes. It's what drives the middle-aged to take lovers, swap spouses perhaps, buy bright, red sport cars. It's what causes poets to write yet another poem about the ocean, the fa-vorite café, fractured life in suburbia, whatever narrow vista circumstance has determined as their own. Sometimes, poets need to cheat on their landscape.

II. Bones

As in Marquez's *One Hundred Years of Solitude*, where Rebeca carries the bones of her parents—her dusty past—around, clacking in a sack slung over her shoulder, poets carry their own pasts with them. However, there are ways to sneak around behind one's landscape's back—long vacations, radical reloca-tions across country or sea. In my case, this time, it's a residency at the Mac-Dowell Colony. Set on 450 acres at the foot of Mount Monadnock, thirty-two widely spread artist studios lay dappling the lush greenery of Frost's New Hampshire woods, "lovely, dark and deep."

I was born in Brooklyn, lived my first five years in Queens. My parents—my new twin sisters and me in tow—moved upstate to New City in Rockland County, an hour and fifteen minutes drive over the George Washington Bridge and up the Palisades Parkway. Back then, in 1965, Rockland was past its heyday as a resort for wealthy city dwellers, as a supplier of brick for building up the burgeoning cities of the northeast, as an origin of fresh, clean ice for the hoteliers of Manhattan. It was still dotted with family farms and apple orchards; streams still held trout; snakes, croaking bullfrogs were expected. I freely wandered the woodlands surrounding Phillips Hill Road, fished the ponds for hours, turned over rocks in the streams, and worried crayfish.

By then it had become a safer, less expensive alternative to city life. The 1955 opening of the Tappan Zee Bridge served as a floodgate that has yet to crank shut. Norwegian contractors had begun the job of converting farms and orchards into developments. Today only two farm-orchards remain, supported largely by weekend, day tripping applepickers; one still grows a little local corn, snatched up quickly at stands and at several upscale markets. It would be a surprise to see a snapping turtle cross my lawn. Black bear and flocks of turkeys may yet be glimpsed from time to time, but only because they've no place left to hide. The bear sightings have become spectacle with a hint of danger, fodder for the *Journal News*. Rockland has become as suburban as northern Long Island and Westchester. It is now a SUV-driven realm of the married with children, of struggling dot-commers and American Dreamers, of straggles of emptynesters not yet fled to Toms River or Florida.

What the place was, what it's become, and how this relates to my situation these past ten years has been the project of my recently completed second book of poetry, *Anticipate The Coming Reservoir*. I've been rattling the bones.

III. Dance

"How can we know the dancer from the dance?" Yeats asked. I don't know. I've attempted to change partners, but somehow I'm still dancing with the one that brung me. Even in the arms of these New England woods I realize, from the poems I've been writing here, that the most intimate dance of all is the one we dance with ourselves. Together on the floor, always; even in sleep, in dreams.

I'm not much of a dancer, awkward and self-conscious, always stepping on someone's toes. I tend toward the role of wallflower. I sit and watch, and there's some jealousy. At such times, the world before me seems washed in the splintered light of a disco ball. Whatever the DJ is playing, it's always the hollow, percussive music of bones. The bones I carry. They want out. They want *Danse Macabre*. Saint-Saens knew. Neil Young knew, too: "When you dance, do your senses tingle? Then take a chance. In a trance, while the lonely mingle with circumstance." I've been lonely in the company of my bones. I want to jump someone else's, to dance with them, my own bag of woe forgotten under a folding chair. I want that prismatic spotlight, the heat, the breathy dance floor whispers. Rockland is a boneyard for the single. It's a relief to be here in New Hampshire; it's an escape, a refreshing dalliance. My second night here, after a fiction reading in the library by a fellow colonist, there was a dance. A very attractive poet DJed. Then she danced. I was a wallflower.

IV. Poetry

I couldn't take it. I picked up my bag of bones and walked the dirt road through blackness to my studio. Mosquitoes whined, sensing the heat of my body bouncing off a filmy, Deet-laced barrier of repellant. I kneeled at the hearth and built a fire, poured a glass of mediocre pinot noir, and sat down at the small desk in the screened-in porch. Minimal ground light makes these woods seem extraordinarily dark to New Yorkers. It seems so to me even though I've left on the light over the studio's front door. It occurs to me to shut it off. More than a dozen moths cling to the screens. I glance up, and I see a single mosquito and a long-legged flying insect whose identification is beyond my entomological expertise. They dash themselves against the bulb, hover a stunned moment, then smack up against the light again and again. It happens here every summer night. It's ordinary. I've left out my notebook and pen. Bones begin to rattle. I identify rhythm; I find it and begin to groove. The music is that of a xylophone. Not Lionel Hampton, exactly, but recognizable music nonetheless. Patterns, structures reveal themselves. Slowly. The whispering begins. Whose woods these are? I think I know now that they're mine, though I've promised myself to another, the girl next door, and I haven't forgotten her. She's in my marrow, and I love her, and sometimes I hate her. We'll spend the rest of our lives together. Suddenly, she's breathing in my ear, flicking her warm tongue for good measure. My attempted transgression has strangely excited her. It excites me, too. So we dance.

62

Ann Hostetler

Sonnets for the Amish Girls of Nickel Mines

I.

He tied their legs together, made them face
the blackboard, released their brothers, mothers,
teachers, then barred the doors with two-by-fours.
Ten pairs of toes lined up in place.
Ten pairs of arms could not erase
a moment set in motion by such error.
Ten starched white caps could not conceal their terror
as ten heads bowed in simple grace.
Where once they took their turns to stand apart
and write a sum or sentence they had learned,
(the unprepared might feel some mild concern),
they now could hear each others' beating hearts
as his handgun called the roll—Mary,
Lena, Marian, Anna Mae, Naomi Rose.

II.

Naomi Rose, Mary, Lena, Marian
and Anna Mae—dressed in white by family
and placed in wooden caskets on display
for last loving looks from friends and kin—
now ride in somber carriages again

past the home of he who took their life away
leaving a family puzzled and betrayed
of all they thought he could be as a man.
Their last journey protected by patrol
—even reporters must have a pass—
they move on to church and grave. We are left
without a verse or story to console
us on an autumn day whose shining grass
reflects the sun, a blue sky of clouds bereft.

III.

A blue sky of clouds bereft, wide open
to receive the innocent. But those who live
must have their explanation; the other five
girls recover in intensive care—again
they'll have to live the moments of their pain
even as their families struggle to forgive
the gunman, receive his widow, kids.
For us or them, life will never be the same.
We wait to gather crumbs of consolation
from what they can remember or will tell
of what's unspeakable: the oldest girl
offering to be shot in lieu of others,
her slumped body found beneath chalked letters:
Unexpected visitors bring sunshine.

IV.

Unexpected visitors bring sunshine:
The covered casserole still oven-warm,
gleaming jars of produce from the farm
home-preserved: peaches, cucumbers in brine,
blackberry jam, hard-boiled eggs stained with wine
of red-beet juice. This red will do no harm.

This giver's knock brings blessing, not alarm,
an offering to those who've lost in kind.
The scattered toys, the silent house awash
in grief that stunned a family unable
to believe what had been done. The Amish
givers ease the unlocked door ajar and rest
the box of food on the empty kitchen table.
Forgiveness is the unexpected guest.

EVERY BUGGY HAS FOUR WHEELS: MAKING "SONNETS FOR THE AMISH GIRLS OF NICKEL MINES"

These sonnets were written rather quickly in the week following the Amish school shooting in Nickel Mines, Bart Township, Pennsylvania, on October 2, 2006. I found out about the school shooting on the telephone when my husband called me on his way home from work to ask if I had heard about it. The phrases "Amish school" and "school shooting" collided in my ear, an unimaginable obscenity. My husband and I both have deep Amish roots. His family lives in Lancaster County, and his parents helped found the Mennonite Church in Bart, Pennsylvania, which they still attend.

Because we now live a thousand miles away in Indiana, the telephone continued to be the primary medium through which we learned of this tragedy. Throughout the next few days, phone calls brought us glimpses of the aftermath. My husband's cousin, who lived in an Amish area about twenty miles from the site of the shooting, opened his home to local Amish people who wanted to learn the latest news from television. His family room was full day and night for the first few days after the event. The Pennsylvania Amish are closely connected: his neighbors are the grandparents of one of the victims.

In light of Amish prohibitions against photography, it seemed ironic that in the first few days after the school shooting the Amish community was forced to watch television in order to learn about their own community. Nonetheless, members of the media, as shaken by shock and grief as the rest of us, used restraint in their portrayal of the news. Thus, for me, the drama unfolded primarily in my mind's eye.

My associations with Amish one-room schools are many. My father, John A. Hostetler, was born into an old order Amish family, but did not join the church as an adult because he wanted to further his education. His career as an anthropologist and cultural interpreter for the Amish kept him in touch

65

with the community, and he involved his family. Visiting Amish schools was a privilege of mine when I was a child, and I often longed to teach in one. Every summer during my childhood I spent a week on the Pennsylvania farm of my old order Amish aunt and uncle. My husband wrote his MA thesis in clinical psychology on Amish schoolchildren. We met each other through his work with the Amish, and the six teachers with whom he worked attended our wedding and made us a quilt for a gift.

One of the women who worked on that quilt, Naomi Huyard, a sister of one of the teachers, was brutally murdered by neighbor boys a few years later. I turned to writing to grapple with the problems of death and evil and began a correspondence with the niece of the murdered woman. I eventually wrote an essay in which I attempted to come to terms with the question that she asked me: "Where was God when Naomi died?" Another of the victim's nieces self-published a book about the tragedy and the forgiveness her family extended to the killers, who are still in prison. Writing can be a form of healing, even though it cannot replace the loss. Through my relationship with the Huyard family, I also knew that forgiveness of the murderer does not mean an end to suffering for the survivors. In the aftermath, the Amish families of Nickel Mines would be dealing with posttraumatic stress, grief, fear, and a shaken faith.

One of the things that makes coming to terms with a violent death excruciatingly painful is that in order to fully empathize with the victim, one must imagine the scene of their last moments. The last minutes of those children's lives haunted me. As the details were reported, my mind wanted over and over again to picture that schoolroom. And because I have been in many Amish schools, and because many Amish teachers are personal friends of mine, I had a good feel for what that schoolroom was probably like. The previous winter I had taken the California poet B. H. Fairchild to visit a local Amish school here in Indiana. He was overcome by the experience, astounded that such beauty, trust, and order still existed in this world—the children in their neat rows, their pure-hearted singing, their drawings and poems neatly tacked to the walls, the motto of the day inscribed on the blackboard.

Now a different kind of visitor had come to an Amish schoolhouse. My precious glimpse of an Amish schoolroom through the eyes of a poet had been contaminated by a demented, gun-toting assailant with pornographic tendencies. At first I resisted my mind's directives to imagine the scene, and then I relented. I realized that the girls needed a witness, even in retrospect, even in imagination. I would honor their pain by allowing myself to stand in their space, in their shoes.

When I learned of the Amish school shooting, I didn't plan on writing poetry about it. However, I had attended a poetry gathering a few weeks before the event that had left a profound impression on me. At "The Resilience of the Spirit" conference at the Guthrie Center in Great Barrington, Massachusetts, poets from such war-torn places as Belarus, China, Cuba, El Salvador, Iran, Iraq, Kurdistan, Palestine, Poland, Rwanda, and Vietnam read the work born out of their struggle to make meaning in the face of war, torture, imprisonment, dislocation, and exile. A few months earlier I had met the poet Marilyn Nelson and made a study of her work, including *A Wreath for Emmet Till*. I marveled at how she had created something of beauty and integrity from the brutal lynching of a young adolescent. What stuck in my mind was the way in which she honored the beauty of Till's life, the fully dimensional human presence that is so often flattened or erased as we grapple with a tragic ending. Again, the resilience of the human spirit shone through.

I rarely write formal poetry for publication, but in this instance the sonnet form allowed me to bear my grief. Marilyn's sonnets gave me the courage to try tackling this difficult subject. Once I began the first one, it seemed almost to write itself. When I was finished with the sonnet, I still wanted to write more, yet I didn't want to relinquish the neat container of the sonnet. Naming the girls seemed of primary importance to me, and I began a new sonnet by repeating their names. As details of the story emerged in the news, I kept finding images to add to the sonnets: the funeral procession, the white dresses of the girls, the Amish neighbors who brought food and forgiveness and offers of help to the widow of the man who killed their children.

Although the details in the poems come primarily from news stories, the images came through a kind of imaginative telepathy, informed by my lifelong connections with the Amish. For instance, I have always had a love of the colorful fruits and vegetables preserved in canning jars, and often an Amish aunt or cousin would wrap a few of those jars in newspaper and tuck them into a cardboard box for us to take on our journey home from a visit. On and off over a period of several days, I sat at my laptop computer in the kitchen in the evenings after dinner, scanning the Internet for news stories, checking on the latest information about the girls, testing the images that formed in my mind for factual accuracy. I continued to write, almost as though a force were speaking through me, until I wove a wreath of four sonnets.

When the sonnets were finished, I showed them to one of my sisters, who told me they reminded her of the four wheels on an Amish buggy, with their rhythm, balance, and stability. The sonnets helped her to bear her grief because they suggested the formal qualities of Amish life, the possibility that its order and regularity and predictability might be restored. Reluctant to publish art stemming from someone else's pain, I showed the sonnets to one of my Amish schoolteacher friends. She was deeply touched and asked for a copy. It struck me that the sonnet, with its formal structure and rhyme, had made the poems particularly accessible to an Amish audience, as Amish-authored poems are always rhymed. I finally decided that it would be appropriate to share the sonnets with a community of readers close to the tragedy and through whom the Amish might have access to the poems. Thus I sent them to the *Mennonite Weekly Review*, the Mennonite newspaper with the largest circulation, where they were published. Later they were reprinted in the *Elkhart Truth*, a local Indiana newspaper in a community with a large Amish population. This honors, I believe, the Amish custom of publishing occasional poetry for the community on the death of loved ones. But there is more.

I haven't been able to think of the Amish girls of Nickel Mines without connecting them to the women and girls in Iraq and surrounding countries who are being subjected to the violence of war. When I first heard of the Nickel Mines shooting and the Amish forgiveness, I couldn't help but think of suicide bombings aimed at civilians and honor killings at women and girls. What forgiveness will it take to restore humanity and freedom, especially for young women threatened by systematic violence? As I lay a wreath at the feet of the Amish girls who died at Nickel Mines, I also lay a wreath at the feet of girls who have died simply because they are innocent, simply because they are girls, singled out as targets. I haven't written poems for them because I do not know their stories or cultures nearly as well. I haven't yet been given the words.

Julia Spicher Kasdorf

Double the Digits

we called the game Jenny made up driving
back roads through West Virginia

at twice the speed on signs. Foot on
the gas, foot on the brake, she'd take

a 25 mile-an-hour curve at 50, triumphant
until something thudded under the hood,

then hissed as we drifted to the berm;
engine block cracked, her dad's Peugeot

left for the wrecker, sold for scrap.
She never could tell him how girls,

16 and 18, could get so bent on speed
they'd ignore an oil light's warning.

When my dad's Plymouth Fury hit 78,
weightless, on a crested curve of Route 136

and nearly flew into the grill
of a soda delivery truck, we swerved

toward a pole on Donna's side then
were gone before the guy hit his horn.

We never said it, but close calls
like that made us see·state troopers

on front porches, hats in hand, moments
before our mothers open the door. Yet

we played that game every chance
we got until college separated us

from our fathers' cars. Jenny divorced,
then married a canoe guide up north.

Because Donna's husband is black,
she can't set foot on her home farm.

And at 35, I can barely stay in the lines
so I keep going back, as if those times,

half a life ago, could explain why some women
get driven by a dumb desire for flight.

MEMORY AND THE PROBLEM OF WHAT REALLY HAPPENED

"But it *really* happened!" I can't stand to hear that defensive whine, as if the test of a poem were how well it can imitate life. If you think about it, real life is not all that interesting, filled as it is with tedious and pointless parts of routine; even the details that may be personally satisfying often carry little meaning for anyone else. Mostly real life consists of one dull or small thing after another, no narrative rise and fall, no symbolic resonance or unity of effect. Life is not literature. And yet for writing to be interesting, it must be believable enough to engage a reader's emotions, or surprising enough to intrigue her intellect; sometimes insight and innovation even meet.

So how to make writing that is realistic without being merely what really happened? Lucky for us, there's memory, that unconscious process that con-

70

stantly shapes raw experience into a story. During the 1980s, research in arti-
ficial intelligence involved studies of narrative because early work in that field
had established that human intelligence is linked to the ability to remember,
and we create memories by making stories. The shapeless nature of what
really happened gets fixed in the mind: First this . . . then that . . . then . . .
then . . . because . . . and so! Much of real life we forget because it is forget-
table. It takes something extraordinary for the mind to begin shaping raw ex-
perience into a story with a beginning, middle, and end. Our minds are
always at work telling ourselves stories so that we can make sense of things.
And often those stories begin with a question that has no apparent answer:
Why is this so?

What is true for the individual is also true for families and communities.
Many of my early poems were retellings of stories that existed in my family as
explanations for why things are the way they are: Why are there no photos?
Why do the ancient aunts feel ashamed? Or, they were explanations for my
own unanswered questions: Why did I lie about what happened to me that
day long ago? The research into human memory turned out to be useless for
creating artificial intelligence; it's impossible to construct a machine that re-
tains information as we do. But I have recalled reading about it because it
helped me to understand how I write. In other words, it provided a story that
explained the way something mysterious works. It also suggested to me that
the stories we thought were true may be merely constructions. If a story can
be made to explain an event, then it must also be true that—with some imag-
ination and will—new stories can be made, and old meanings can change. In
this way, the poems we write can alter the ways we understand and order the
world, and that is a very exciting prospect, indeed! The test of human intelli-
gence is our ability to change our minds, to revise the meaning of that which
we believe to have really happened. Let me show you how it works for me, a
poet who, I must confess, nearly always writes from what really happened.

In composing "Double the Digits," a real life experience prompted my
recalling a memory that then triggered a poem with a few surprising turns.
One afternoon, I found myself driving on twisting, Pennsylvania back roads
with a friend from the west where roads are straight. At one point, clutching
the door handle, he said he was surprised by the speed at which I was taking
those curves. It hadn't occurred to me. I explained that I'd spent a lot of my
adolescence driving back roads with the radio blasting, sometimes playing
double the digits. As I heard myself telling him about Donna and Jenny, high
school friends I hadn't thought of in years, and the time we cracked the Peu-
geot's engine block, I felt a certain resonance, or excess of meaning. I knew
then or maybe later that I wanted to write that memory in order to find out
what it could say about now. I didn't want to analyze or think too hard about

71

it beforehand; I just wanted to write and see what would show up in the language and images.

The first draft (unless you consider the first draft my oral telling) came out in one solid run, a story that was shapeless but largely intact, scrawled onto a long yellow sheet of legal pad paper. To make the raw material of memory into a poem, I had to follow and reinforce the meanings that surfaced.

Double the Digits (first draft)

We called the driving game.
Maybe Jenny made it up as we flew through back roads in West
    Virginia twice
the speed limit. You can do it,
foot on the gas, foot on
the break, taking a curve marked 25 at 50.
We didn't hit anything then, but heard a blast
under the hood, then a hiss as we drifted to the berm.
The engine block busted and her Dad sold his Peugot for scrap.
I don't think she ever could explain how we could ignore
the oil light, two girls ecstatic and hell-bent on speed. Doubling
    the digits
at 16 and 17. Now coasting on the mid-thirties
I keep thinking of the weightless way
my Dad's huge Plymouth Fury
lifted over the crest of a country road at 70 and almost
wrecked into a soda delivery truck, too fast for the man to hit
his horn, almost swiping the telephone pole on Donna's side.
Times like that we'd get silent, as if we could see it all, down to
    the state troopers standing on our mothers' porches, hats in
    their hands.
Still we kept at it until we left our father's cars.
Jenny divorced, then remarried a canoe guide up north.
Donna lives with a black man who is not welcome at her family's
    farm.
My own life, too close to collapse into one flat line,
just keeps returning to that time, our dumb hunger for flight.

A quick comparison between this first draft and the final version shows that the basic information of the story—the details of what really happened—remains constant, but decisions of craft guide and enable the narrative to accrue meaning. Words change to sharpen images, capture sensation more precisely, and enliven the colloquial tone of voice. To begin with, the title reading into the first line gives the reader a sense of taking a curve too fast. During the course of revision, the poem's basic shape shifted from one stanza, to three paragraph-like stanzas, to the final choice of couplets, which advances the idea of doubles—as it refers to the game and to the girls/women at two points in their lives. A strategic line break—"separated us/ from our fathers' cars"—hints at the gravity of matters that will emerge by the end of the piece. The word *flew* is removed from the beginning of the poem so that *flight*—both senses of the word—is stronger in the last line. The assonant "dumb hunger" is replaced by the alliterative "dumb desire" because desire reinforces the poem's erotic tone, and the final lines ring with rhymed words that also share a kindred sense in this poem: women/driven and desire/flight.

Borges at the Northside Rotary

If in the following pages there is some successful verse or other, may the
reader forgive me the audacity of having written it before him.
—JORGE LUIS BORGES, foreword to his first book of poems

After they go to the podium and turn in their Happy Bucks
        and recite the Pledge of Allegiance
and the Four Truths ("Is it the Truth?
                Is it fair to all concerned? Will it build goodwill
and better friendships? Will it be beneficial
        to all concerned?"), I get up to read my poetry,

and when I'm finished, one Rotarian expresses
        understandable confusion at exactly what it is
I'm doing and wants to know what poetry is, exactly,
                so I tell him that when most non-poets think
of the word "poetry," they think of "lyric poetry,"
        not "narrative poetry," whereas what I'm doing

is "narrative poetry" of the kind performed
        by, not that I am in any way comparing myself
to them, Homer, Dante, and Milton,
                and he's liking this, he's smiling and nodding,
and when I finish my little speech,
        he shouts, "Thank you, Doctor! Thank you

for educating us!" And for the purposes
    of this poem, he will be known hereafter
as the Nice Rotarian. But now while I was reading,
        there was this other Rotarian who kept talking
all the time, just jacked his jaw right through
    the poet's presentations of some of the finest

vers libre available to today's listening audience,
    and he shall be known hereafter as the Loud Rotarian.
Nice Rotarian, Loud Rotarian: it's kind of like Good Cop,
        Bad Cop or Buy Low, Sell High. Win Some,
Lose Some. Comme Ci, Comme Ça. Half Empty,
    Half Full. Merchant Copy, Customer Copy.

But in a sense the Loud Rotarian was the honest one;
    he didn't like my poetry and said so—not in so many words,
but in the words he used to his tablemates
        as he spoke of his golf game or theirs
or the weather or the market or, most likely,
    some good deed that he was the spearchucker on,

the poobah, the mucky-muck, the head honcho,
    for one thing I learned very quickly
was that Rotarians are absolutely nuts
        over good deeds and send doctors to Africa
and take handicapped kids on fishing trips
    and just generally either do all sorts of hands-on

projects themselves or else raise a ton of money
    so they can get somebody else to do it for them,
whereas virtually every poet I know, myself included,
        spends his time either trying to get a line right
or else feeling sorry for himself and maybe writing a check
    once a year to the United Way if the United Way's lucky.

The Nice Rotarian was probably just agreeing with me,
    just swapping the geese and fish of his words
with the bright mirrors and pretty beads of mine,
        for how queer it is to be understood by someone
on the subject of anything, given that,
    as Norman O. Brown says, the meaning of things

is not in the things themselves but between them,
    as it surely was that time those kids scared us so bad
in Paris: Barbara and I had got on the wrong train, see,
        and when it stopped, it wasn't at the station
two blocks from our apartment but one
    that was twenty miles outside of the city,

and we looked for someone to tell us how
    to get back, but the trains had pretty much stopped
for the evening, and then out of the dark
        swaggered four Tunisian teenagers,
and as three of them circled us, the fourth
    stepped up and asked the universal ice-breaker,

i. e., Q.: Do you have a cigarette?
    A.: *Non, je ne fume pas.*
Q.: You're not French, are you?
        A.: *Non, je suis américain.* Q.: From New York?
A.: *Non, Florida.* Q.: Miami?
    A.: *Non, une petite ville qui s'appelle Tallahassee*

dans le nord de. . . . And here the Tunisian kid
    mimes a quarterback passing and says, *Ah,*
l'université avec la bonne équipe de futbol!
        He was a fan of FSU sports, of all things
so we talked football for a while, and then
    he told us where to go for the last train.

Change one little thing in my life or theirs
    and they or I could have been either the Loud Rotarian
or the Nice one, and so I say to Rotarians everywhere,
    please forgive me,
my brothers, for what I have done to you
    and to myself as well,

for circumstances so influence us
    that it is more an accident
than anything else that you are listening to me
    and not the other way around,
and therefore I beg your forgiveness, my friends,
    if I wrote this poem before you did.

THE DELIBERATE TRANSFORMED BY THE ACCIDENTAL

I chose "Borges at the Northside Rotary" to end my book *The Ha-Ha*, and I picked it to close *The House on Boulevard St.* as well. I also end with it frequently when I give readings, for the simple reason that it turns poetry away from the smart aleck on stage and back to the reader.

I also like to read this poem aloud because, if the acoustics are right, I can hear it working in a way that doesn't always happen. Usually, though, the acoustics aren't right, which is why often I rely on intelligence provided by Barbara Hamby, the poet I've learned most from as well as my wife and thus a regular audience member when I'm giving a reading.

Take November 12, 2007, for example: that night, I read "Borges at the Northside Rotary" at Manhattan's New School as part of the National Book Awards ceremony. My book *The House on Boulevard St.: New and Selected Poems* was a finalist that year—it didn't win, but being a finalist means it was one of the five best poetry books of 2007. Believe me, I've had worse things happen.

Anyway, Barbara was sitting in the audience, and later she told me that, when I read the poem's last line, the man behind her said, "My god, he pulled it off." Pulled what off, though? And how?

To me, art is the deliberate transformed by the accidental. So are foreign policy and astrophysics and gourmet cooking and courtship, for that matter, but let's stick to art for the moment. In this case, the deliberate part consists of me going out to the Northside Rotary Club in Tallahassee to give a reading, as I do every once in a while; the gentlemen and ladies of that group have

78

me read a few poems, talk to them about what poetry is and how it works, and answer their questions.

Now professors being the snarky types they are, if somebody said, "Here's a poem about Rotarians," you'd be right to expect that it would be a hip and disdainful piece about a bunch of golf-playing businessmen, and probably many living poet-professors would write that way. Well, I'm not one of those. The Rotarians I know are to be envied, and I'd probably be one if I weren't so jealous of my free time, because they spend their time doing deeds that change the world far more than the swimming-pool Marxism embraced by many of my learned colleagues at the university.

So here I am a few years back, reading some forgotten poem to these guys, and things go more or less the way they usually do. When the Nice Rotarian shouts out his thanks, I don't think a thing of it; in addition to their other fine qualities, Rotarians—well, most Rotarians—have old-school manners and are courtly to a fault.

But when the Loud Rotarian starts up, instantly, and in the middle of whatever poem I'm reading, I say to myself, "Oh, great: here comes another one." Because I see on the spot that a little whitecap has appeared on the sea of poetry, and that part of my job is to get out of its way and let it turn into a good-sized wave on its own.

After all, a reversal in fortune is no fun if you're trying to win somebody's hand or simply stage a successful picnic, but it's the writer's lifeblood. Aristotle calls this *peripeteia*; rhetorician Kenneth Burke calls it "Trouble With a Capital T." But the best explanation belongs to John LeCarré, who says that "The cat sat on the mat" is not a story, whereas "The cat sat on the dog's mat" is.

Okay, so with great deliberation, I look over my work and take a shower and comb down my cowlick and drive my battered Corolla out to Northside Rotary to read my poetry, and the next thing I know, the Loud Rotarian—the accident—provides the start of a poem that will become "Borges at the Northside Rotary." And that's how things went outside of the poem. But inside the poem, there's another accident, a built-in one that disrupts the deliberate flow and transforms it into something worth listening to, if the guy sitting behind Barbara at the National Book Award ceremony is to be believed. And that's the story about the French teenagers.

Now I happen to think this is a pretty good story. First of all, it, too, involves something deliberate (trying to get home) as well as accidental (missing our stop), and everybody loves to hear stories about what a dope you, the storyteller, are. I mean, who'd expect to go to another country and end up out in the boonies at a rundown train station after midnight and run into a bunch of menacing teenagers only to find out that one of them is a fan of your small-town football team an ocean away?

The fact is, though, that I needed to interrupt the Rotary Club thread with something, meaning anything. I've had thousands of misunderstandings, and I can think of a hundred I could have plugged in here instead of this one. Robert Bly calls the transition from one thread to the next a leap, and I could have leapt to any other lily pad in the big pond of poetry. Lately I've been writing a lot of music journalism, and one thing you learn there is that there doesn't have to be a tight fit between music and lyrics or even between one musical passage and another. In fact, there shouldn't be a tight fit: if the song's going to work, it has to surprise us.

So there you are in the audience, and the smart aleck on stage is reading his poem, and he's going on for a while, and suddenly he stops talking about the Rotary Club and starts talking about France, and that part's starting to get a little stretched out as well, which gives you time to ask yourself: is this guy going to bring it back around to the Rotary Club? And he does! And it seems as though the poem's over.

But then comes the surprise, because the poem's not really over. There's one more line to go, and in that line, the smart aleck brings his listeners back to that Borges epigraph you forgot about long ago. And there's some clapping, and you go off to the reception, and people are telling the poet he did a good job, which is also what they'd say if he'd gotten up there and read the first ten pages of the Tallahassee phone book, and he thanks them and tries to get through to the bar before they run out of red wine, and you make a mental note to stay away from the chips and dip that are being monopolized by a guy who looks as though he has an unusually contagious case of pellagra.

But if you're the poet, and you planted a spy in the audience, you might find out later that, when you finished reading the poem, somebody said, "My god, he pulled it off."

Clown Baby's Summer

At the beach Clown Baby comes out of his own miniature tent—red and white stripes, little big top. He toddles. He hasn't learned the ringmaster's language, and his laughter is an odd barking through red painted lips. The white of his face is like a moon. He can juggle the sippy cup, bottle, and two breasts. Correction: his face is white like a breast. In a bathing suit he looks ridiculous, but just see him in a ruffled shirt.

THE NATURAL BIRTH OF CLOWN BABY, OR HOW I CAME TO MIDWIFE, FATHER, AND WET-NURSE A PROSE POEM SEQUENCE

First off, let it be said that I had never been interested in writing a sequence of poems before this, had always been wary of the poetic project as being too pre-scriptionary for my own creative process. Ultimately, I want language to sneak up on me, compel me to write, and what's written comes out of that language—that place where words and rhythm and image all meet. Usually, it's a line, but in the case of some of my prose poems, it's come in the form of a title, such as "Early Experiments in Ingesting Fire" or "The Museum of Pastries," phrases that, once said, got my imagination running with somewhat absurdist possibilities. It's in such moments that I find impetus for prose poems.

This ear for a phrase I think is crucial to all poets, and it's one that I learned from Thomas Lux back when I was a poet-in-training. Tom used to say he found titles by finding those two- or three-word phrases that inherently generated tension. Consider some of his book titles, such as, *Memory's Hand Grenade*, *Half Promised Land*, *The Drowned River*, and you can see what I'm talking about.

81

But when I was in the water of the Grand Traverse Bay that summer afternoon seven years ago, my wife a few feet away, I'll admit that I wasn't thinking about prose poems or about whatever book it was that lay on the beach blanket. I was thinking about the summer program for high school writers at which I would be teaching, and whether I'd get another trip to the beach before I had to go back home. When my wife pointed to the shore at a small red-and-white striped tent only a few feet from where our towels waited, and asked "Hey, what's that?" I'll admit to some flippancy. "It's a tent," I said. "A little big top."

"Oh," she replied. "What's in it?"

"Clown baby."

As soon as I said those two words I felt suddenly colder. "Clown baby." The tension between the two generated all sorts of questions: A baby that is clown? A clown that is baby? A baby born clown? It was as if the words had static electricity coming off of them, and I had been shocked. Within minutes I was wading through the water, heading to where I knew a pen waited. And the tent.

In the tent it turns out *was* a baby—the tents are made so that infants can sleep at the beach or the park and be protected from sunburn. It was an ordinary baby—no big shoes, not even a multicolored outfit, and surely no clown hair. My Clown Baby, though, was already being birthed by the time I saw this real child of the little big top. And the prose poem stayed true to the experience.

I drafted the prose poem quickly; so enamored was I with that phrase that I wanted to work on it. When I finished "Clown Baby's Summer," I thought I might be done with it, but the fact is the expression *clown baby* kept haunting me. I liked to say the two words together: "clown baby." I worked on the prose poem some more until it felt both finished and unfinished simultaneously. In this neither-nor-ness, it generated more energy, more spark. "Where did clown baby come from?" I wanted to know. "And what might happen to him?" Still, I had no clue what to do next. This prose poem, after all, was done.

And it felt so complete to me that I showed it to some folks at the Controlled Burn Seminar for Young Writers, for now I was finished with vacation and down to some serious teaching and spending time with other writers. Mary Ann Samyn, my wife at the time who taught with me, loved the poem's whimsy and seriousness, and she, too, couldn't resist saying "clown baby." Debra Marquart, after listening to it, asked how clown baby was conceived. I had no idea, so she suggested that clown baby's mother was inhabited by the spirit of a trickster-god; she also told me a story about how some tribal women (were they Native Americans or Aborigines or Africans? I don't remember now) believed that pregnancy occurred when a spirit entered the body, and

that the women could even tell the location and moment when it happened. As she talked, "The Conception of Clown Baby" became the new phrase. It generated more static energy. My hairs were standing up being so close to it.

But I'm much too carnal for a virgin birth, and although I believed Clown Baby already to be mythical, he hadn't yet taken on some of the surrealist-messianic qualities he would later acquire the more I wrote about him. So I fused the sacred and the profane, the cosmic and the carnal, if you will.

The Conception of Clown Baby

Because she wouldn't laugh. Because in the circus tent that summer Saturday, she clapped & ate cotton candy, but wouldn't laugh. Because she's scared of clowns, the soul of Clown Baby came to her. When she made love with her husband that night, she laughed when she came, and kept laughing and didn't know why.

Suddenly there was more to come. The problem with sequences though, I realized—having read so many that frustrated me—was the risk of them becoming parodies of themselves, of sounding too similar. And so I rode that clown baby energy for a while, writing a few other clown baby poems over the next several weeks. By then writer friends who knew what I was working on (and some of my Controlled Burn students, too) would contact me with ideas: clown baby gets a puppy, clown baby and the kidnappers, clown baby and the stacking toy. . . . Oh, so tempting.

And ultimately not tempting at all.

As I would work on more of these over the course of five years, I maintained a few rules. One: clown baby always had to be just that, a baby. Clown toddler isn't as funny. Ditto clown kindergartner. And in adolescence—we're all clowns. Two: I was in no rush. I refused to write another clown baby because I could. Rather, I would only write a clown baby prose poem when compelled. Three: That the first rule of genesis of clown baby is/was the right one: He was conceived of the tension in language, of the friction found between *clown* and *baby* when placed in that order, side by side. "Baby clown" doesn't cut it. And in that tension, in that neither-nor-ness, is the energy of the prose poem itself, of all those hybrid creatures of myth: the centaur, the Minotaur, the satyr. The clown baby series could not be lineated poems. They are inherently prose poems. Those nice square cloths that could be his blanket as he sleeps in his tent at the beach.

Mary Linton

Up Late With Loons

Four loon calls at 2 a.m., as the rump
of a rainstorm wiggles to the east.
Soon more drops knock against the taut
skin of the rain fly, over and over,
like the persistent nagging that you've
forgotten something. Not something
important like your beloved's shoe size.
More like why the prophet Isaiah
walked mother-naked through the streets
of Jerusalem for three years.

Or was that months? Whichever, the sun
must have been fierce. What did they use
for skin cream back then? For a while you try
to remember what the message of all that dusty
flaking deep-pink flesh could have been.
Wasn't it a righteous gripe about the way
his country's cream didn't care for widows
and orphans? Anyway, you're sure
that if this keeps up, you won't be prophesying
tomorrow. And it does: the nose of one storm
closely following the tail feathers of another
in a way that's not so hygienic.

MAKING PEACE

I am fifty-two years old and I still love camping out. The perfect spot is anywhere the concentration of people is reduced enough to allow the welling up of quiet and the proliferation of stars. It is a pleasure to be awakened at 2 AM by the rustling of unknown critters, the call of owls, or a coyote nose inches from my nose. It is a delight when hummingbirds attack me in my bright blue sleeping bag on a dazzling Rocky Mountain morning. But I am fifty-two, and the ground just isn't as soft as it used to be.

My last camping trip was for the express purpose of writing poetry. Poetry takes space and focus, and we were giving ourselves the elbowroom. I could hear the clicking sound of my brain shutting off the parts that worry about things outside of immediate needs—paper, pencil, and the above mentioned space. So, it did not surprise me that when I was awakened by rolling thunderstorms, lightning flashing like strobes, and the calls of a pair of loons on the lake, a poem came up for air in my soggy brain caught in that dark moment between rumbles.

The storm images came first and set the tone for the poem. With those mildly barnyard pictures, it wasn't going to be a fully serious poem. Once the rump of one storm was headed east, I knew the nose of the next was on its way. But there in the second half of 2006, and the second half of a second disastrous imperial presidential reign, my mind was never far from the mess in Iraq and Afghanistan, in Lebanon and Israel, and the messes threatened in Iran and North Korea. I got on a slow train of thought starting in a tent in foul weather, traveled to bombed-out homes and flimsy refuges made out of blankets, and got off on the Iraq platform. Though, lord knows, I could have traveled on to Kabul or Darfur.

I have a lot of Bible study under my belt. I consider myself a recovering seminarian, lured irrevocably away by the siren song of science to invest my life in wetland ecology and conservation. Given that history, when I find myself in Iraq, between those two magnificent rivers, I can't help but think of the weeping willows (*Salix babylonica*) under which some psalmist wept after being carried there by an army that so recently had decimated Israel. The Israel caught in a squeeze play between Egypt and Assyria and Babylon that greatly predated our current work. My mind crawled from there to those three prophets who chronicled that history: Isaiah, who warned but died before the doom he predicted; Jeremiah, who wrung his hands as the armies closed in and conquered; and Ezekiel, who was forcibly removed to those *Salix babylonica* where he dreamed the future and the return. I knew that one of them publicly lay on one side for several years, then switched to the other, as a visual sermon. Since my backpacking pad was feeling a bit thin, it seemed like a good story to connect my space with the prophet's space. I thought it was Isaiah's story. I hoped it was Isaiah, because Isaiah was the one who was most focused on the behavior of his own country that would lead to its demise, namely treating the dispossessed and downtrodden, the poor and un-protected, so shamefully. He repeatedly talked specifically of widows and orphans, but they were merely the emblem. This was long before "buyer beware." This was an expectation of high integrity and compassion, or as the Dali Lama says, "Good Heart." I wrote the poem down after breakfast the next day and moved on to the next. The interior of the poem looked something like this: "More like why the prophet Isaiah lay/on his right side for three years,/only to flip to his left side for another/ year. Was it about how to treat widows/ and orphans. . . ."

When I got home from the trip, I started to comb the writings of the three prophets for the aching hip-and-side story. Ezekiel was the prophet who lay on his side for all those months. Ezekiel didn't talk that much about what got him to Babylon; he talked about getting out. The months of lying about were part of a prediction of when he could return to his beloved home-land. What do I do now? I could keep the story and somehow make Ezekiel fit my homily, or I could find a good story from Isaiah and make it fit the poem. I toyed with leaving the story attached to Isaiah, but that science side of me demands precision, and I couldn't do it. I chose to keep Isaiah and use his own story because Ezekiel just isn't my man. He's too Blake, too science fiction, too upper class for me. None of this was a moral dilemma I wanted to attach to writing poetry. The last thing I wanted to do was to add insults to the folks who love that beautiful region of the world and call it their home-land. Not political correctness; maybe just a meager attempt at Good Heart.

Revision always includes word play: improving assonance and alliteration, removing adjectives and adverbs and putting them back in, substituting words to make the tone more consistent. I did my share until the poem was ready enough to go into an envelope addressed to an editor.

Shara McCallum

Penelope

Lemon rinds in the dried brook-bed,
Fireflies in the face of uncertain evil—

all, like me,
suffer the occasional drought.

Outside my window,
no islands of foliage

block my view to the shore.
No river noises trickle in.

Listen, after years of waiting,
I tire of the myth I've become.

If I am not an ocean,
I am nothing.

If I am not a world unto myself,
I have to know it.

The Biography of a Poem

"Penelope" began in my journal on May 5, 2003. The first draft was titled, "The Unreliable Narrator Speaks to Her Audience." By the second draft, written that same day, Penelope had entered the picture and the poem had acquired alternate titles: "The Unreliable Narrator Speaks to Her Audience" or "Penelope Refigured." The uncertainty partly reflected my discomfort with the self-consciousness of the first title. More important, the shift signaled that Penelope would become one of *the* principle factors in my revisions to the poem.

For me, the process of revising a poem involves not only figuring out what I'm trying to say about a given subject but also becoming aware of whom is speaking. Penelope, a figure of myth I'd long been interested in but up to that point in my life had been unable to imagine fully, seemed capable of the kind of utterance that comprised the first draft's opening lines: "I know I am losing you now / when I most need you to hear me / most need you to know that I am / speaking to you across this barrier of time." I knew a feeling of desperation, coming out of a sense of not being heard or truly seen, was what I wanted the poem to convey. Locating that sentiment within Penelope's story and delivering the poem from her viewpoint would, I felt, give me and the poem greater direction.

Formally, the poem began as a single stanza but in the second draft migrated to quatrains, which were present as a unit of sound and rhetoric to my ear in even the first "block" version. By the time I moved from my journal to the computer (draft three, on May 9), I changed the stanzaic structure again, trimming it to tercets. Playing with stanza lengths has, for the past ten years, been a revision tool to help me refine language. Determining a fixed length is not an arbitrary process but one governed by the dominant stanza length I see emerging as I revise the poem. Working with a defined stanza forces me to make difficult decisions about which images, words, and lines are best for conveying a poem's idea or feeling.

I like focusing on stanzas as well because doing so allows me to regard the poem's structure as a whole: I like considering how I want the poem to move down the page and through time. Not the time of the event—if there is one in the poem—but, rather, the duration of time it takes for a reader to read and experience the poem. The word *stanza* originates in Italian and means "little room." By extension, I imagine the poem as a house. The length of each stanza reflects how long I wish the reader to dwell in each room and how much space I want to offer between these rooms. To my mind, the couplet offers the most space for pauses and reflectivity in a poem, the tercet a bit less, and so on. Because I favor a controlled pacing and tempo, I almost always select a fixed stanza length. If I deviate from the pattern, this happens via enjambment across stanzas or as a more marked shift at the end—a truncated, single-line stanza on which I might close the poem, for instance.

Regarding its stanzaic structure, "Penelope" was published in tercets in the Fall 2004 issue of the *Antioch Review*. The opening lines retain the idea present in the first draft, though much else from early drafts went by the wayside as I concentrated on building a new context for Penelope's story and voice. Since the *Antioch* version is quite different from the final one, it bears citing in full:

Penelope

I know I am losing you now
when I need you to hear me most,
speaking across this barrier of time.

Listen, if I am not an ocean,
I am nothing. If I am not a world
unto myself, I have to know it.

Lemon rinds in the dried brook-bed,
fireflies in the face of uncertain evil—
all, like me, endure the occasional drought.

Out of the ashes of another,
I rise to fill the void of anyone leaving,
of anyone who has been left.

Troubles wouldn't even know where to find me,
replete with my comic and pathetic flourishes,
my jingle and jangle, splash and pizzazz.

Outside my window, no islands of foliage
block my view to the shore.
No river noises trickle in.

Nothing left
but me scratching out these words,
waiting for your message in return.

While I had worked on this poem for months before sending it to *Antioch* and felt fairly satisfied with it when I submitted it to the editor, after its publication there were things that continued to trouble me. When I began putting together my third book, weaknesses in the writing became glaring to me and the question of where the poem would fall in the manuscript arose. Both of these considerations affected my later revisions of the poem, which underwent another ten or so drafts over the course of the next two years. I won't go into detail about every change but will highlight the major ones and the thoughts—as I remember them—that accompanied my choices.

First: the title continued to be in flux. In November 2004, it became "Dear Country." At the time, I imagined the poem as part of a long sequence I was writing that addresses aspects of Jamaican political history and my family's personal history during the 1970s. The title change, I hoped, would make it possible for the poem to "fit" into that sequence. By late 2005, I dropped that idea and went back to "Penelope," the rightful speaker and referent point for the poem. The poem also became the prefatory poem in the manuscript, the first two sections of which contain poems centered on motherhood, marriage, and domesticity.

Second: I began to be ruthless with the poem, cutting any line or stanza that seemed weak or disconnected in the least. Stanzas one, four, five, and seven went onto the chopping block in their entirety. I remember thinking with the fourth stanza, for example, that the phoenix really had no business being in the poem and that the writing in that stanza was fairly abstract—so, time to go. Some choices were harder, though: in the fifth stanza, for instance, I really loved the line, "my jingle and jangle, splash and pizzazz," but felt it disrupted the tone of the poem too much to warrant inclusion. Reluctantly, I let it go. (As a side note, I am fairly meticulous about keeping drafts of all of my poems, principally so I can go back to earlier versions of a poem if I make a wrong turn with a revision, or so I can hold on to language that might not fit a given poem. The line in question here later made its way into a long poem, "From the Book of Mothers," the writing of which partly overlapped that of "Penelope.")

Once I had eliminated more than half of what had comprised the *Antioch* version, I was left with a muddle of language that could not be reassembled in the old way. Thinking again about structure, tempo, and pacing—and how best to deliver Penelope's despair—I went to couplets and rearranged the lines considerably. What resulted was the final version, a poem I'm happier with for its concision and for the way the speaker's emotion builds and changes inflection. The poem begins with a series of images, which I think renders it less emphatic in tone at the outset than is the case with the earlier, published version. First comes the scene of a modern-day Penelope, cast in and invoking her Caribbean landscape; then she moves to a more declarative mode, contesting the image of herself as presented via "myth." Three years after the poem began, on May 23, 2006, it came to rest in its final form.

Dinty W. Moore

revelation

boot unlaced, discharged
the hiker's slender foot is drawn
     down

to cold grip of copper water
Blue Hole Creek's determined gurgle
     no other sound

but perhaps, a snap,
a twig,
     leaf falling

falling water, laurel highlands
autumn daylight
     a woman hiking

boot unlaced, foot drawn
cold copper, utter stillness

     she dips the other

The Poem Stripped Bare by Her Author

As someone who spends the majority of his writing time trying to compose coherent prose—fiction and nonfiction—the act of writing a poem is all about subtraction. It often takes me thirty words to say what can be said more sharply in three. On my worst days, it takes me three hundred words. So, I subtract what isn't necessary.

The poem "revelation" is five years old and even now I'm not convinced it is done. The genesis was a trip to the Laurel Highlands with a number of undergraduate honors students and a fortuitous stop along Blue Hole Creek. You can't beat that name. Of course, before the subtraction can begin, the challenge for me as a poet is to slow down enough to really see, to freeze-frame the individual moments, to strip away my preconceptions and perceive what is actually in front of my senses. Thus, a brief poem about a woman's foot, the sounds, the light.

Early attempts to capture those moments on the page tried to make too much of the experience. Despite knowing better, I found myself attempting to drive home some point about nature, about stillness, and about the magnificence of simple observation. But of course that's an inherent contradiction. How can one drive home a point about simplicity?

So this version, stripped bare, ends with the second foot entering the stream. That seems to be the only point I have to make.

Erin Murphy

Covetous

After Eamon Grennan's "Start of March, Connemara"

You ask how the gulls find the right angle in the gale,
how they adapt to the current and let it take them

the way they were going. I could ask the same of you:
how do you find *thumbed* and *wind-scumbled,*

thrusting them together like lost lovers,
letting them glance off each other, polished stones

on our tongues? Or *glitterwings making their mark,*
a dance linguists call the *fricative,*

a word I love because it is what it means,
unlike *palindrome,* which resists mirroring itself

and sends me, instead, to a girl I knew in college,
the one from Glenelg—*g-l-e-n-e-l-g,* the same

forward and back. She had hips that looked good
in boy jeans and a way of making the professor

believe she'd done the reading when she hadn't
even bought the book. Do you see what just happened,

how I started in your lyrical world of shorelines
and wave-peaks and wound up recording

slumber party giggles through a thin wall? Your gulls:
maybe they don't harness the wind after all.

Maybe they give in to each gust and forsake their plans,
having learned long ago to want what they have.

COVETING THY NEIGHBOR'S POEM

Spring 2004. I was sitting on my sunporch reading the latest issue of the *Kenyon Review* and in it Eamon Grennan's poem "Start of March, Connemara." From his poem:

> *. . . Two white gulls, wing-tilted,*
> *are surfing the sou'wester. How do they do it, finding the right*
> *angle in the gale and—angels of the shiverblast—adapting to it,*
> *letting it take them the way they were going?*

I suppose this was the image that struck me first, and on a philosophical level I was considering its antithesis: what if that's not the way they were going? What if they just pretended that's what they'd wanted all along? Of course, I was thinking more about human beings than gulls. I have a high school friend who'd always planned to go to graduate school. Instead, nearing forty, she's a real estate agent because she finds it so fulfilling to "help people find their dream homes." I hope this is true. But I can't help but think of it as justification for having sacrificed her own dream.

Back to 2004. The gull/destiny connection was on my mind, but so, too, was the fact that I found myself envious of the knack many poets have for the meticulously crafted image. How was it that other poets could mold tightly woven gems of poems while mine always sounded like stream-of-conscious conversations you'd overhear in a Greyhound station? Other poems were honed and controlled; mine felt like they "need[ed] a girdle," as I wrote in my poem "Does This Poem Make My Butt Look Big?"

The idea had been rattling around in me for some time, perhaps for as long as I'd been writing. And since the Bible says nothing of coveting thy neighbor's poem, I seized the opportunity to dwell on the idea after reading

98

Grennan's poem. Perhaps I was emboldened by the fact that Grennan himself was writing in response to Elizabeth Bishop's poem "The End of March." It was like the old Breck shampoo commercial: "They told two friends, and they told two friends, and so on, and so on. . . ."

Here's my original draft:

Covetous

After Eamon Grennan's
  "Start of March, Connemara"

You ask how the gulls do it,
How they find the right angle
in the gale, adapt to it,
and let them take them
the way they were going;
I could ask the same of you;
~~the way you~~ How do you find thumbed
and wind-scrambled, letting them
glance off of each other,
polished stones on our tongues?
~~Or glittering marks that mark~~ what
linguists call the fricative,
a word I love because it is
what it means, unlike
palindrome, which (should
~~be spell the~~ itself forward and back)
(refers to (be a) mirror of (g) itself)
resists mirroring itself ~~and it reminds me instead~~ even though
~~it to a still ___ in call___~~ reminds but does remind me
of my friend D. who ~~went who grew up in~~
~~to~~ Glenelg ~~high school~~
g-l-e-n-e-l-g, the same
forward and back.
She had
hips that looked sexy in boy jeans
and hair that never needed combing.
She ~~asked permission~~ to sleep with
~~Any ___~~ and a way of ~~really~~
the professor ~~that~~ she'd done the reading
when she hadn't even bought the book.
Do you see what just happened?, how
I ~~started aloud in your~~ world of ~~lyrical~~
shorelines and wave-peaks and ended

Bishop
same rainy
linguistic fricative
palindrome

up ~~how, ~~ that ~~high~~
in the stuff of Cosmo,
not poetry.

your gulls: maybe
they ~~wind~~ they don't
harnessing the wind
after all. Maybe
the wind is determines
twi-birds' fate and
~~The maybe~~ the birds
~~unlike us,~~ learn to
want what they have.

Maybe the birds
have adapted have learned
to ~~just~~ give in,
~~learning~~ to want
~~what~~ they have.

not only to coast
on what they

Maybe
the wind determines
the birds' course
and the birds
give up ___
learned long ago
to want what they
have.

And here are some reflections on the changes:

"You ask how the gulls do it. . . ." This was the opening line until a friend pointed out that it sounded like the birds were copulating, *à la* Whitman's "The Dalliance of Eagles." I use this example with my students to stress the importance of getting objective feedback on your writing; sometimes we writers are so aware of what we mean that we lose sight of what readers may think we mean.

"She had hair that never needed combing and once asked permission to sleep with my ex." I was trying to characterize this enviable and self-assured girl, but these weren't the right images. The boy jeans and book were. I also toyed with "looked sexy in boy jeans," but ultimately preferred the assonance of looked/good/book.

"I'm up here, chest-high in the stuff of *Cosmo*, not poetry." *Cosmo* sounded at once too old for the speaker's mindset and too dated for the poem, so I settled for the slumber party image. After hearing me read "Covetous" recently, a friend suggested that *Slumber Party Giggles* would be a good title for a book of poems. I think she's right.

". . . unlike palindrome, which should spell itself forward and back." This was way too telling. And too dull and clunky. I decided "which resists mirroring itself" worked better metaphorically and aurally. Plus, I ended up using the "forward and back" line later with the actual palindrome.

"Maybe the wind determines their fate" (and variations). I had an idea early on for the final line (the wanting what they have, as opposed to having what they want), and this was one of many unsuccessful attempts at working up to the ending. I typically rough in an ending at the beginning of the drafting process. It's a backwards way of working, I know, but it's not so different from the way I live. I like a loose plan for the day, even if the plan changes. Likewise, the endings of my poems are always subject to spontaneity, to that friend who calls and says, "There's a matinee in ten minutes—if we leave now, we can sneak in during the previews."

I was satisfied with the final revisions to "Covetous," and so, too, was the most important reader, Eamon Grennan, who wrote to me that poem ran "a good mile beyond its inspiration." This is high praise from a poet whose work I greatly admire.

A version of this essay first appeared in a *Southeast Review* feature called "The Cutting Room Floor," in which writers discuss the deletions they've made in the editing process. In writing and revising this piece, I find myself making the same kinds of revisions I make in writing a poem. It occurs to me that there could be another "The Cutting Room Floor" for "The Cutting Room Floor," and so on and so on, like the Breck commercial. Or perhaps, like the deleted *Cosmo* reference in my poem, that allusion is too dated, in which case, I'll cut it. . . .

Mary Rose O'Reilley

The Third Winter

Their implacable names:
Classen, Boelke, Fricke. . .

The girl from the next place over
brings a line of dried fish,

knowing the child died.
Every day, the wife sits

mostly in silence,
letting the windows

hold her in.
No one under these shingles

theorizes. Sometimes a poem
in the newspaper brought from town

tells them how sad they are,
or gives them a look at the hayrick,

frost on the sill. She tacks it up
in the milking parlor:

someone has seen their lives.
The house, she thinks,

is a body, heart on the second floor,
stomach just above frost line.

In the dugout, that first winter,
he entered her over and over,

thinking of rooms he would build
over the new bed,

thinking the house would have arms.

THE WILD HORSE

The most useful thing I believe about writing poetry—or at least the most useful to me—is *the mind seeks coherence.* I often advise writers, stuck in a draft, to "trust your mind." By mind, however, I don't mean the thesis-generating or outlining organism, but rather, a kind of wild horse that bears us along in the dark. This horse knows how to get home. In the process of composing, I go through month after month of riding in the dark, hanging on to the mane. It seems to me important not to stop, not to intellectualize, not to psychoanalyze the process too soon. Maybe later. I fetch up, gasping and out of breath.

Writing poetry is what passes for spiritual practice in my life. If the phrase suggests cool young women in leotards on the cover of yoga magazines, I can't deny your experience, but, for me, spiritual practice is a daily attempt to face reality as it is: comic, tragic, silly, mysterious—and I get there on horseback or bear-back or sometimes donkey-back, but seldom by tranquil meditation. I write at a brisk pace for long periods of time till I sense that some unconscious process has worked itself out, and I try to trust my mind to present me with a coherent, interpretable pattern. For the moment.

It's the act of discerning pattern that yields a sequence of poems, but, more important, some measure of knowledge. One addresses this material with the strategies of a good therapist or literary critic; amidst the detritus kicking around in any life, *what's repeated, what's emphasized?* By detritus, I mean the accidentals of life: the garden one tends, the political moment, the friends and animals with whom one shares the house.

102

As I turn, just now, to a few hundred pages of writing from the last two years, I begin the canny and cool part of the writing process, more satisfying and serene than riding through the dark. The acts of interpretation and translation I now undertake require a respectful demeanor; I must not push or slash or force the data into conformity with some imagined ideal of a poem or a life. I am not usually happy with my raw material. My drafts are quite different from what I dutifully try to put into the world. But I've learned that what I "dutifully try" to communicate is often the product of a false persona, created to please. Thus, it should not surprise me that my poems are sometimes chaotic, cruel, violent, and inclined to shake their tiny fists at the order of the universe. The task, as Prospero surrendered to it at the end of *The Tempest,* is to repeat at least a Shakespearean prayer: "This thing of darkness I acknowledge mine."

As a teacher, I try not to make a lot of judgments about my students' work, and, similarly, the phrase I bring to my own revision is *I notice.* . . . This sentence invites self-understanding rather than self-defense. As I look now at the work of my last long ride, I notice that, for an outdoor person, these poems are remarkably bound up in the history of houses and barns, rooms, enclosed gardens, and constricted spaces. There is a lot about renovation, scrubbing the floors, and washing clothes. Ghosts, angels, and other unspecified presences inhabit the spaces. Husbands and wives have a hard time in these rooms, and when they get it right, it's often because they are out birding, or daring to do some unfathomably difficult task that is nearly beyond them—or because they've grown old. I've given this new collection the working title *Calling Them Home.* "Well, of course," says my music partner, "that sounds like a hymn." It's also a kind of exorcism. And, because the unconscious loves games and silly puns, let me note that there are a lot of dogs in these poems, with names like Pookie and Muffin, names that I'd never yell out my own door. My dignified border collie will not deign to review these poems.

"The Third Winter" is not an autobiographical poem, although people who interpret dreams teach that every character in a dream might be considered an aspect of the self. There are dreams we dream as a race, as a people, and poems are waking dreams of this kind. The literal history out of which this poem rises, as I only realize in writing about it, includes a scrapbook I inherited when my parents died, kept by my great aunt Ruth (who once gave me a baby pig of my own). Ruth and her husband, Bill, farmed near Kenyon, Minnesota. They had no living children; two had died tragically, one of a burst appendix during a storm that had washed out the bridge, the other from smothering in a corncrib. They were a fierce old couple who kept some distance between them, as though (my grandmother said) each blamed the other or himself. Ruth's scrapbook was full of sentimental poems, cut out of the

103

local paper, about old times on the farm and babes in the woods ("someone has seen their lives")—infinitely more banal than Ruth's own stories, had she been able to tell them.

Although I used to think of the revising process as rational and cool, I've lately begun, to honor a little more the inchoate nature of our collective dreams, to leave the poems a little rougher, a little, as one critic wrote, "snowed-in." In my youth, I was on a mission to redeem art from the obscurities of modernism, to write clear, lapidary poems; this I considered a communitarian responsibility. I didn't want readers ever to feel tricked or flummoxed or foolish in front of any of my work. But I think that the contemporary world finds poetry unimportant, and few people know how to study it or find the task worth doing; for the poet, public inattention can be liberating. For those few readers who want to move into a poem and live there, I leave more to the critical imagination. I don't want them to ask, "What did she mean?" but rather, "What would this dream mean if it were a dream of mine?" Because, I hope, it may be.

Lee Peterson

Anniversary

—for Hamed Efendi

On the day they buried you—no—
the night before—it rained.
As if to clear something—
to clear the throat of God.
     (To wash his feet as he asks us
to wash our own.)

The day before, men with hammers
and undyed wood, mounted lists of names—the dead
     to bury
and those already in the ground.
On white—a number to each—a plot.

     On the day itself our dignitaries spoke
        —a volley of sound—
     amplified, their apologies
     broke between the hills.

Mud swallowed the day.
Women held their heads. And men
bowed—it seemed
—for miles, a hand along the grass, folded,
     folded. Raised.

105

ANYTHING WORTHWHILE

My first book of poems, *Rooms and Fields*, was a series of dramatic mono-
logues set during the war in Bosnia in the early 1990s. To write that book, I
read and read—histories, survivor interviews, an ethnography of a Bosnian
village, court transcripts and legal documents, a long out-of-date book on
Balkan folk traditions, a graphic novel. I began all this research as a graduate
student in 1999, four years after a cease-fire and the Dayton Accords offi-
cially ended the war in Bosnia. With the exception of a few late additions,
some poems and some revisions, most of *Rooms and Fields* was written with-
out setting foot on Bosnian soil.

As I write that last sentence, recalling the many times I've said it aloud, I
feel a familiar (albeit waning) twinge of doubt or even a little embarrassment.
But this doubt about how my work would be seen and judged has abated sig-
nificantly since the project was so well received, from its infancy in a graduate
school workshop to its life as a book. Outside affirmation of the work at every
stage certainly encouraged my pursuit of it. Yet I still found I needed to chal-
lenge my own insecurity throughout the process of writing *Rooms and Fields*
with the belief that in writing, as in life, fear (of failure, of falling on your
face, of what people might think) should never be a reason not to do a thing.
In fact, maybe fear is the best reason *for* doing something. That, and the will-
ingness to put oneself in the position of being surprised, and of surprising
others, proved useful guides and guards against inhibition.

One of my greatest fears in writing the book was of how the poems
would be received by Bosnians themselves, by those who had, in fact, lived
through the war. At the time I embarked on the project, I knew no one from
the Balkans firsthand. Then, as time passed, I met people from the region
through one connection or another—initially through teaching ESL at a
small college outside New York City, my job at the time. I subsequently met
many Bosnians, both here and in Bosnia, through the work itself.

At some point, despite their academic origins, I knew I needed to expose
the poems in *Rooms and Fields* to the people I was encountering who had ex-
perienced what I had only imagined and studied. Yet I was nervous to do so,
fearful both of their reactions and the possibility that I'd simply somehow
gotten it wrong. Ultimately, the poems and I were met only with wonder and
gratitude. (Sentiments I returned in kind.) And never more so than when I
went to Bosnia for the tenth anniversary of the massacre at Srebrenica on July
11, 2005, a trip that led to the writing of "Anniversary," the poem in this
anthology.

Srebrenica is a small town in the mountains of Eastern Bosnia. Before
the war, its main industries were salt and metal mining. The town's name
means "silver mine." And with all the lead, zinc, and iron ore in the earth and

106

water, it was also a thriving spa town. Since then, however, it has gained an international reputation as the site of one of the grimmest acts of mass violence to take place during the war in Bosnia.

A United Nations-designated "safe area" during the war, Srebrenica became the place where thousands of Bosnian Muslims sought refuge and protection. And although the town was surrounded by the Serb Army, a small Dutch peacekeeping force did provide a period (and the illusion) of safety. In July 1995, however, the Dutch were overrun, and the Serb Army captured the town. What followed was the worst single act of genocide on European soil since the Holocaust. On July 11, 1995, some eight thousand men and boys were murdered in the town, a nearby village, and the surrounding hills. The incident was an international embarrassment, to say the least, and the outrage that followed was part of what led the international community to abandon its position of neutrality. Military intervention, a ceasefire, and the Dayton Peace Accord followed within months.

Across the street from an abandoned battery factory, where a large number of the executions took place on that day, now stands a memorial. There is a monument, but the site is essentially a graveyard for the dead whose bodies or partial remains have been found and laid to rest. Many remains are still being identified so many years later. Many more are still missing. One of the missing is Hamed Efendić, the husband of a woman in whose house I stayed while I was in Srebrenica for the week. Fazilla Efendić also lost her teenage son, Fazo, on that day.

At Fazilla's house I slept in what had been Fazo's room. A large picture of him, in glasses and smiling slightly, was perched on a desk by a window. One afternoon, drained from travel and a visit earlier in the day with a photographer friend to a mass grave, I stayed home with Fazilla and looked at her family photo album. The pictures made me feel close to them and to her. Fazilla's daughter, Nirha, who arrived from Sarajevo later that day, is my age and was finishing her own graduate studies at the University of Sarajevo. Nirha's father, Hamed, had been an architect, like my own.

In the days that led up to the anniversary, countless mourners streamed into the tiny town. Journalists arrived and set up shop. Politicians made their way into the narrow eastern Bosnian valley. Preparations had been taking place all week. Each day I went to the site and saw the graves being dug for the burials to come, the lists of names being put up, the men working shirtless in the hot sun. Low marbled fountains lined the edge of the field for the ritual washing of feet and hands. On July 10 it rained and stormed all night.

The next day, the field, the graveyard, and the memorial site were a bath of mud. People jammed through metal detectors into the fenced space. Richard Holbrooke spoke over an echoing sound system. There were conference-style lectures inside the factory lit with bright television lights. There were women in scarves, buses, imams, the Serbian president, and the Bosnian president. I saw a backpack standing unattended and grew nervous. There had been threats. And the week before, officials reportedly removed enough explosives from where we were all standing to blow up the entire memorial area and any number of people in it. Despite all the chaos, there was silence between the speeches. There was prayer.

It took me a year to commit any of it to paper, a year to the day. To commemorate the anniversary of my going, of the massacre, I wrote this poem. Any earlier would have been too soon for me. How to honor the dead and the living I'd encountered? It wasn't harder than the work I'd done for my book, writing about all those people I'd met only on other people's pages. But it was different. As more of a witness to and participant in an event of such magnitude and massive emotion, I experienced a sense of preciousness and a lack of distance.

My mentor from graduate school, Suzanne Gardinier, recently sent me an e-mail in which she said, "Anything worthwhile, anything alive, takes time." I find it always takes me time to write. I'm pretty slow. Maybe the time, the looking back, allows a thing to be whole in a way that it never was. Memory lends *and* removes clarity, accuracy, and potency, so the poem and its truth have their own life in the end. Yes, time and, again and always, a willingness to face fear. These were crucial elements in the writing of "Anniversary," these and the real lives of the people in that valley on that day—both present and past—the many lives, including my own.

Greg Rappleye

Orpheus, Gathering the Trees

after the *Metamorphoses* of Ovid, book X, lines 86–112

When love died the second time,
he sang at dawn in the empty field
and the trees came to listen.
A little song for the tag alder,
the fire cherry, the withe-willow.
The simple hearted ones that come quickly
to loneliness.
Then he sang for the mulberry
with its purple fruit,
for the cedar and the tamarack.
He sang *bel canto* for the quaking aspen
and the stave oak;
something lovely for the white pine,
the fever tree, the black ash.
From the air he called the sparrows
and the varieties of wrens.
Then he sang for a bit of pestilence—
for the green caterpillars,
for the leaf worms and bark beetles.
Food to suit the flickers and the crows.
So that, in the woodlot,
there would always be empty places.
So he would still know loss.

IN THE WOODLOT

I had been writing long narrative poems about the American painter Martin Johnson Heade (1819-1904), who is often identified with the Hudson River School of William Merritt Chase, John F. Kensett, and Frederic Church. In particular, I was focused on Heade's work during the Civil War, when he journeyed to Brazil to paint hummingbirds. Heade's plan was to have his hummingbird paintings chromolithographed on the great presses of London or Paris, to have the lithographs bound under the title *Gems of Brazil*, and to secure his fortune by selling the folios in a subscribed limited edition under the sponsorship of Brazil's Emperor Don Pedro II. Heade failed, though much of his work from that era survives, best represented in his painting *Tropical Landscape with Ten Hummingbirds* (1870).

My Heade poems were beginning to look like a collection, and it occurred to me that I ought to leaven the reader's slog through the narratives with more lyric poems, both about Heade's work and with ones that might associate Heade's failure with some larger, even mythological context. I began, as one will do, to think about Orpheus.

Every poet knows the story of Orpheus and his failed attempt to bring Eurydice back from the underworld. Perhaps *too* many people are familiar with that part of the story. What is not so fully known is the life of Orpheus afterwards—his attempts to compensate for the loss of his wife. So I began to explore—rereading *The Greek Myths* by Robert Graves and various translations of the *Metamorphoses* of Ovid. I was looking at paintings, particularly Jean-Baptiste-Camille Corot's *Orpheus Leading Eurydice from the Underworld* (1861), in which Orpheus, lyre held resolutely before him, is shown leading Eurydice, not out of the rocky depths (the way one might traditionally think of their journey from the underworld), but through a swampy, springlike landscape of trees just coming into leaf.

I live on the edge of a woodlot, drained by a small creek. My woodlot is a scraggly collection of brambles, poplars, red pines, cedars, and wild undergrowth, where once had been a working blueberry field. At the margins of the quarter section, some of the blueberries remain in orderly cultivation, but behind my house, there is only what some might see as a wasteland, what comes after a working field is plowed under and abandoned. I was spending a great deal of time that spring staring into the trees.

It is said that not long after Orpheus looked back, against the command of the gods, and lost Eurydice, the poet went into an empty field and used his lyre to gather the trees around him. Here's how Ovid tells the story, in Allen Mandelbaum's magnificent translation of the *Metamorphoses*:

There was a hill and, on that hill, a glade
an ample span of meadow grass, a plain
that was endowed with green but had no shade.
Yet when the poet, heaven-born, would play
on his resounding lyre, shade on shade
would seek that glade. Together with the tree
of the Chaonians, these came to listen:
the tall and leafy oak, the tender linden;
the poplar, shape that suited Helios' daughters;
the willow, most at home near flowing waters;
the virgin laurel, beech and brittle hazel;
the ash, so fit for fashioning spear shafts;
the silver-fir with its smooth trunk, the myrtle
with its two hues, and the delightful platan;
the maple with its shifting colors, and
the water-loving lotus, evergreen
boxwood, as well as slender tamarisk;
and with its deep-blue berries, the vibernum;
and bent beneath its acorns' weight, the ilex.
You, ivy, with your feet that twist and flex,
came, too; and at your side came tendrils rich
with clustered grapes, and elm trees draped with vines;
the mountain-ash, the pitch-pine, the arbutus
red with its fruits, the pliant palm, the prize
of victors; and that pine which tucks its boughs
up high to form its shaggy crown—the tree
dear to the mother of the gods. . . .

I began to look through field guides and nature books, making lists of
tree names, sorting for the most interesting varieties, for folk names, for leg-
ends, cross-sorting for the types of trees that might be found in my swampy
woodlot, the plants that might begin the process of overgrowing a field-gone-
fallow. As I winnowed my list, stopping now and again to leave my desk to
look into the undergrowth, I saw that there were dead and empty places
among the trees, and thought that something in my soon-to-be poem should
account for that emptiness.

Keith Ratzlaff

Sunday

for Treva

It's a jittery morning,
mild threat after mild threat:
Hawks wheel and drop,
a black Labrador running loose
has brought the neighborhood
dogs to chorus. In the cedars
a panicky cardinal
can't stop and can't stop
his hysterical tik, tik, tik.
Then a siren climbs
its own red pole until
it might be tornado or terrorists
or just, this time, noon.
Even on Sunday there's alarm
at having misplaced half a day.
I'm away from home. Not far,
not lost, in no danger
except the long-shot kind
of West Nile virus or
the plummeting fragments
of a satellite. My wife
is home reading the paper,

113

drinking coffee, unconcerned,
I hope. Then the chickadee's
splintery "look at me me me,"
thin and urgent as if
the worst has happened.
But he's really just talking
to his mate, and now
he switches to his other voice—
"feebee"—the one reserved
just for her: two notes
that drop a major second,
the first, short, descending step
of an old scale we know.
I recognized it today
as the whistle my wife and I use
when we're separated in crowds
or across a lawn, when we want
the other's specific attention.
It's a selfish sign, which at first
means only, "Hey, look over here."
But acknowledged, it's softer,
and means what Mecca pilgrims mean
when they chant to God at Mount Arafat:
"*Labaik*—I was a hidden treasure
and I wished to be known. Here I am."

An Essay with Two Short Lectures: Revising "Sunday"

I'm not someone who usually keeps his poems locked away for nine years (as I think some Greek wag recommended) to see if they stand the test of time. The fun of writing poems at all is in the process, in the generative kick they give us. If a poem can't work its way to a satisfying conclusion in three or four months—and I know poets whose release time is much shorter—it's more often than not time to move on. My guess is most poets feel this way. But most poets, I'm still guessing, also have a file for those drafts and snips of language we hope will come to something but that almost invariably never do. This is the story about one of those drafts that turned into a poem I like.

114

I had been in Chicago, away for month. I missed my wife and was ready to go home. It was April, the light was clear and white, and I spent some time one morning watching two chickadees flit around a hole in a tree making what I imagined was a nest. I recognized the chickadee call—two clear, descending notes—as one similar to a little coded whistle my wife and I use to find each other in crowds. The two naturally came together, and I scribbled this notebook entry:

Near Easter

Today the chickadee sings
its two falling notes
which are mating call
and lament. And the man
with big ears who lives
on the corner shouts at me
from his porch: "Do you know
the name of that bird?"
Reader, go beat the rugs,
it's spring. Do something
useful. This is a stupid story—
about love, and so barely true—
about an old man
whose face in this light
is a question mark,
some unknown letter
of the alphabet,
who has heard this song
for sixty years and never asked
before—a sound he says
he's imitated in malls
to tell his wife "Here I am."
She has always looked up
and found him. "Chickadee,"
he says, "the bird of love."
And who knows what's on
his mind? And who would
argue its resurrection?

115

Any reasonably bright workshop beginner could have helped me sort this out. Those chickadee lovebirds are front and center where they should be although why they are lamenting, I can't say. But for some reason, I've invented a cartoonlike old man to carry what are obviously my own feelings about chickadees (who are monogamous I found out later), and love, and married life. That leaves me free to be the flip, knowledgeable narrator of the story, the one who gets to ask the questions, but who doesn't have to get involved. The poem stalls—at least for me and I'm the one who counts at this point—because I'm trying to put my emotions into an invented character's mouth. The title seems to point toward a resurrection (with terrible Fisher King/Viagra overtones it seems to me now), but I kept it anyway in a thin manila folder with Working Poems scribbled on the tab.

Seven years later I was in Chicago again, walking through a similar neighborhood on a Sunday morning. This time it was late summer 2002, close enough to September 11 for terror to be in the air, but there were other big stories in the headlines that month: It was the first summer of West Nile virus in the Midwest; the Bush administration's war cries for the UN to condemn Iraq were at their most strident; a Russian satellite was falling out of orbit and looked as if it could come down anywhere in the world. Like Chicago. The events of that morning walk are the first half of "Sunday": dogs barking, a siren blaring for seemingly no reason, cardinals and chickadees singing their alarm.

The chickadees took me back to the fragment of seven years earlier, and their song now becomes the pivot of the poem. In this version I have a better idea about just who the romantic lead is in this movie: me. As the speaker I'm willing now to own the poem.

I don't have any drafts to show this, but I was stumped for an ending, and the poem sat for a while without the last four lines. Then one night reading myself to sleep, I came across these lines in an essay by Ziauddin Sardar about the *hajj*, that pilgrimage to Mecca that all Muslims make once in their lives if they can: "Each pilgrim says simply '*Labaik*'—'Here I am'—in the knowledge that each is individually heard, individually known, individually valuable, distinct, and particular. 'I was a hidden treasure and I wished to be known.'" With the new poem unfinished on my desk, how could I not have been struck by the echo of that phrase from the scrap of seven years before—"Here I am"? I didn't jump out of bed, as I sometimes do when a line of poetry strikes me, but dog-eared the page and fell asleep. The next morning I used the lines from the essay nearly verbatim and the poem was done.

Any ending seems magical for the writer who needs one, and I was convinced for at least a couple of hours I had been "meant"—by who or what I couldn't say—to read that Sardar essay. I'm happy the last lines acknowledge the political tensions of the times, even if they aren't really overt in the poem.

To have the resolution of the poem be in some way the answer to the world's issues of love, of the pilgrim's delight at the end of a long road, pleases me.

The drawback (although it depends on what you think of Simon and Garfunkle) is that "Here I am" is also the last line of "The Only Living Boy in New York," and I tend to sing the lugubrious ending of that song—I'm singing it now—when I read the poem.

You could argue this isn't really a revision. Maybe. But the moment of recognition I had as I was reading and falling asleep that night seems to me a continuation of the day seven years earlier watching chickadees building a nest. William Stafford would have merely called this kind of paying attention "receptivity." Too often we teach and practice revision as an exercise in cutting, probably because of the weekly and semester time pressures of writing workshop life. Revision for me is less about contraction or consolidation than it is about connection. I don't believe there's a thin poem in every fat poem waiting to get out.

Two things, then:

1. When we make poems—when we link sounds and words hoping for what used to not-so-quaintly be called beauty—we put in motion a series of expectations like a chord progression. These can stay caught and unresolved in the poetic ear like cicadas waiting for years to tunnel out and say, "Here I am."
2. Probably no one could actually have helped me come to the final version of "Sunday" unless his advice had been to wait or be quiet or grow up. In the end the big revisions aren't about the poem at all, but about poets and the times in which they live.

117

Jack Ridl

Repairing the House

We will learn the house can live
without our changes. We will

listen to its language. The cracks
along the stairway—they are sentences.

We will read what they say
when we go up, again when

we walk back down. When we
leave our sleep, our beds will hold

our place as the floor creaks under us.
If we fix the broken window, then

we will open it. The other windows
rise on their tracks; that's enough;

one staying shut, tight, will still bring
light for any day, the others the breeze.

And we will learn to be with the ivy
straying along the back brick walls,

twisting itself into the mortar, each spring
a chunk or two falling into the holly.

We will feel a draft under the porch door.
We could block the cold from sliding

toward our feet. Instead, we will wear
socks, ones you made, while we sit facing

each other, reading on the sofa, its stuffing shifting
under us, the pillows giving way to what is left.

THE POEM AND I HAVE A LITTLE CONVERSATION
—by Jack Ridl and "Repairing the House"

This is a little conversation that attempts to reveal what happens most of the time when I try to write a poem. I start off, usually with some notion or twitch of an idea. That then becomes a title out from which I start writing. In this case the notion was the need to do some repairs on our house and the negative consequences of not attending to these needed reparations. I wrote a draft. It dealt with how not fixing the house could hurt a marriage. The following "conversation" came about as I listened to the poem trying to tell me what I hadn't realized. The poem, any poem I try to compose, is invariably smarter than I am. But I'm stubborn; every time, I want to have my way. Then finally I start to listen. Here's the kind of thing I usually hear.

JACK: Ok. Done. Got down exactly what would happen if I don't make those needed repairs to the place.
POEM: It's all negative. The consequences are all negative.
JACK: Of course they are.
POEM: Of course they are?
JACK: Yes, of course they are.
POEM: You're sure?

(The poem is often like some Zen master all but whacking me behind the head.)

JACK: So what are you saying? You're telling me there are positives to not repairing the house?

POEM: Yes.

JACK: And I assume that you're implying that there are also negative consequences if I *do* repair the place.

POEM: I don't know about negatives, but there are certainly valuable things that won't happen if you make these repairs.

JACK: Help me out.

POEM: Oh, come on. Well, how about this: Can you two live without making those changes?

JACK: I guess we could.

POEM: No, I don't mean put up with not making them. I mean live.

JACK: Oh.

POEM: Look at me! What if the cracks are gone? What if you can no longer hear the creaks in the floor? What if you don't fix that one window; what will you notice? What if you don't fix the wall where the ivy is growing?

JACK: The place will go to hell!

POEM: Put me away. Go for a walk with the dog or rake some leaves or take a nap or read some poems or—just put me away.

PAUSE

POEM: You're back.

JACK: I am, and. . . . (Jack starts writing again.)

POEM: See?

JACK: Shut up.

POEM: Yes! That's it: don't fix the draft under the door. Yes, put on socks, those socks she made for you. Yes, see? She's putting on socks, too. Look at me! Sit on the sofa together. That's a good sound by the way, "sofa." I like what that sound feels like.

JACK: I like ending with those socks and sitting together on the sofa.

POEM: Well . . . I uh . . . .

JACK: You think it's cheesy.

POEM: Well . . . .

JACK: What do you want?

POEM: C'mon, can't you feel it? Comfort. I want to feel that.

JACK: And that's not cheesy?

POEM: That's not what I meant. Read me.

JACK: You want it more comforting. Ok, how about some pillows?

POEM: Well, sure, pillows are comforting but it's still—

JACK: Cheesy.

POEM: No, you got rid of that, but it's resolved.

JACK: So?

POEM: You know better.
JACK: Pillows give way. If they give way then . . . .
POEM: You got it. Now, finished?
JACK: A poem's never finished; it's—
POEM: Abandoned. Ready to abandon me?
JACK: Yep.
POEM: What did I end up being about?
JACK: A poem's always about a lot of things.
POEM: I say that it's about the socks.
JACK: The poem is about the socks?
POEM: Well, yes. And socks come in what?
JACK: All sizes.
POEM: No! These socks. These socks come in pairs.
JACK: So?
POEM: The socks.
JACK: The socks.
POEM: C'mon. You can't be this blind. What do you call two socks?
JACK: A pair.
POEM: Duh. And what does that have to do with me?
JACK: Oh my god! A pair of socks. Two pairs of socks. The couple is each wearing a pair of socks. The couple is on the sofa. Not fixing the house is to—
POEM: You got it!
JACK: To fix the couple. To re-couple!
POEM: You're kidding me? To re-couple?
JACK: Yeah.
POEM: To re-couple? What have you been talking about doing?
JACK: Repairing the house.
POEM: Uh huh. Repairing. Repair. To re-—
JACK: Pair! They are re-paired!
POEM: Genius. Now, what's wrong with the structure?
JACK: Nothing.
POEM: Well, ok. In one sense nothing. It's in one solid block.
JACK: Right. They are together, solid.
POEM: Think about *couple*.
JACK: Couple.
POEM: Couple.
JACK: Two.
POEM: Yes. Two. A pair is two, a couple is two, is a—
JACK: Couple, couples, oh my god, couplet! It can be in couplets.
POEM: Genius.

Steven Sherrill

Coming Out of Caliban

For three hard hours
I watched my daughter watch
this kink-backed boy snort and hiss—
supplicate his scaly curses
to the will of booted men.
I answered, with all
the truth I could muster,
her questions. Calmed,
as best I could, the storm
of her young fears.
But when the wretched monster
scuttled across the proscenium
dragging the irrefutable centuries behind him—
when he slithered right
up to the precipitous curtain call
then rose on a truer man's two legs,
winked, then smiled, then bowed, and we
both fell head-over-heels into
the moment—I knew
soon enough, my sovereign role
would be done.

ARE YOU WATCHING?

Here, now, at forty-five years old, I've come to some conclusions.

The first is that I love being forty-five years old. Time seems to have loosened the vice-grip, that throttling hold one applies to all things deemed desirable. The years have (recently anyway) unwound, by a few generous cranks, the blinding sense of urgency that permeated my earlier decades. *Got to go. Got to go now. Got to. Do this. Do that. Do. I want this. I want that. I want.*

Too, the balance between testosterone and good sense has tipped, just enough, in favor of the latter. The ego becomes more recognizable no matter the mask. Anger. Lust. Arrogance. Et cetera. And therefore, from time to time, less able to hold sway over the moment.

Too, I've stumbled into the willingness to be who I am fully, without apology. To live my life as I want, unerringly. But to do so means facing the great risk of becoming a complete narcissist—and the even greater risk of seeming so to others. While I sometimes struggle with the degree of compassion (for myself and for others) required by my choice, I have always strived to work in good faith, work out of goodness, even when the work embraces wickedness and meanness. I've tried to follow a path dictated by love.

What does this all have to do with writing poems?

It's been a topsy-turvy, circuitous journey, from birth to the nearly half-century mark. Hurtling recklessly here, mired in doubt and fear there. Somehow along the way, and mercifully early on, I noticed that when I allowed writing to be my compass and guide, no matter how treacherous the path, the world seemed right. The trip itself became more bearable, if not enjoyable.

So for years I've clung to this buoy, this act of writing. And gained much along the way. I've come to trust the direction, the process, even when the goal or the destination is unseeable. I used to write a lot of poems. Used to chase the ideas down and strong-arm them into submission. I write novels now and wait for the poems to find me. It wasn't a conscious transition, only following the path faithfully. And now, when they come, these rare birds, these poems, I don't try to control them. Nor possess them. It's like they stop in for a visit. And as it most often happens, their visits coincide with a moment in which I have something to learn, something to see. I need only to pay attention. *To pay attention. To pay attention.*

David Shumate

Revising My Memoirs

I'm taking out all references to mosquitoes. And volcanoes. I'm eliminating 1959. I'm giving my best friend red hair and a lilt to his walk and having him move to the neighborhood from Scotland instead of Cleveland. I'm adding another installment of fireflies to the second chapter and making my grandfather live another three years so he can see his favorite baseball team win the pennant. In this newly revised edition my third grade teacher refers to me affectionately as Plato and the bully who plagued me all those years develops a debilitating stutter. At present there are twelve references to you. But I'm thinking about consolidating them to three. In one you will be singing soprano in a nocturnal choir. In another you will be trimming a young girl's hair. In your final appearance you will be knocking on my door, naked under your raincoat. This time I will not have just stepped out the back door to buy a bag of plums.

CUTTING LOGIC LOOSE FROM ITS TETHERS

Poetry is a strange endeavor. You go snooping about. Sticking your nose into other people's business. Turning your soul inside out. Then you huddle over a paper for hours to give voice to what you have learned, and in the words of the great Uruguayan writer Eduardo Galeano, ". . . try to find words that are better than silence."

✸

I take a rather blue-collar approach to writing. I get up early. Write for a few hours. Take a coffee break. And write some more. I don't feel full until I've written a poem.

✸

My poems arise from many places. I hear the word *Babylon*, and it's as if I'm hearing it for the first time. Its enchantment works on me. My father enters the scene. He's had too much to drink. Somehow there's a sword in the attic. And a poem begins to take shape. Soon the orange flags of Babylon will be blowing in the breeze. But I don't know that until much later.

Or I realize I've lived most of my life in the Bible Belt, and I find myself writing a poem in which each Bible in this region weighs a hundred pounds.

Or I drive across Kansas beneath the full July moon and think of drawing a picture of Jesus. Soon the inmates of an asylum take over the task.

✸

So it starts with an image. A word. A regret. A passion. Or a hundred other things. Then I cut logic loose from its tethers and surrender to intuition. Sometimes this leads me in circles. Other times it takes me to the core.

✸

I am guided by Hemingway's admonition to find the first true sentence and build from there. Sometimes I pile a dozen lines up only to realize that the last half have lost their veracity. So I set those aside and rebuild from where I lost that luminous thread.

✸

As the poem is taking shape, I distill the language, removing debris, testing the rhythm of the syllables, searching for the opportunities I let slip by.

I revisit the poem in the days and weeks to come. I look for gaps, fresh words and images that were too stubborn to reveal themselves the first time through.

I reach for what is elemental in the subject of the poem. I seek words and images that possess the honesty of stones. Of water.

I want the poem to glow in the dark.

✸

Sometimes strands of humor seep in. This is fine with me. I open the door of the poem wide enough for humor and pathos to enter at the same

126

time. It's like those ancient Greek masks the first thespians wore. When the comic comes to center stage, he's holding the mask of tragedy behind his back.

∽

The common perception of writing is that it is a grueling process that takes its toll on the writer. Some claim that it is ultimately fatal. They present the corpses of tormented writers as circumstantial evidence.

My experience is different. Sometimes, as the pieces of a poem are taking shape, I feel momentarily whole. As if the senses, the mind, the intellect, the ego, and some spiritual core have fallen into synchrony.

This is a seductive feeling. I return the next morning hoping a poem will lead me there again.

I hope the poem conducts the reader on a similar journey.

Aaron Smith

Christopher Street Pier (Summer)

Waves

The glass of New Jersey
has shattered (sweep it up!)
& scattered
     the distance
     between

          there

          &

          here.

    ꝏ

Wish

That ugly people would
put their clothes back on

that the jock
in the red T-shirt (blowing up)
(white band of underwear) (skin!)
would pull his shirt off

129

& walk walk
in front of me

∽

Cell Phone

I shouldn't have answered—

talk can ruin
a perfectly good day.

∽

Happy

Man on his back in the
grass. Hair on his chest like

grass.   (One nipple)
                        (Two nipple)

Rolling   rolling   over.

    Hairy armpits . . .
       (yum)

∽

Lovers

A man picking grass
off another man's back.

∽

130

Holy

Hamburger wrappers in the water, plastic
plates, napkins soggy,
dissolving—

the Hudson is littered with trash

The man smelling his armpits (grace)
The woman scooping dog shit (grace)

flipflopsflipflopsflipflops (!)

ༀ

Evening

The construction cranes in New Jersey lowering
an orange-y, egg yolky sun . . .

AGAINST SOLITUDE

I wrote "Christopher Street Pier (Summer)" in 2007 during one of the loneli-
est summers I've had since moving to New York City. My best friend aban-
doned our friendship, and an elusive man had left me spending my evenings
and weekends wandering around the city waiting for something to happen. I
was looking for the interpersonal equivalent of winning the Publishers Clear-
ing House sweepstakes: you have to enter to win. I thought if I showed up for
life, something would happen. I'd also been thinking how all the times when
I've felt as if I've had nothing, I've had poetry. I'm not implying poetry as
therapy. I'm implying poetry as an important, time-consuming practice that is
worthwhile and a good distraction for when you don't feel like wallowing.

I was about halfway finished writing my second book of poems that
summer, and I started to wonder what would happen if I actually showed up
for poetry (as I was trying to do for life) instead of waiting for it to come find
me. I usually find myself waiting for inspiration, for an idea to present itself,
but I was curious to see what kind of momentum I could build through

131

routine. I bought a green notebook at Duane Reade, and four days a week all that summer I left my miserable job at the Modern Language Association, took the 1 train to Christopher Street, and planted myself at the Factory Coffee Shop to write.

I didn't take my laptop because I wanted to see what writing by hand would do to my work. Since I am a poet who is genuinely obsessed with the body, I was curious to see if moving my hand across the page would add a different sort of feeling to the poems, something more physical to the language I put on the page. When I write on a computer, I can't move forward if there is a typing error; therefore, I spend a lot of time backspacing and wasting time during a first draft. When I first started writing, I wrote by hand, but I abandoned that for a computer (mostly writing undercover during work hours). When I wrote by hand, I found (remembered) that I would just scribble through and keep going, not losing the energy. I know this is basic creative writing rhetoric (don't stop and edit), but it's easy to forget sometimes where we started.

After writing for a couple hours, I would walk down to the Christopher Street Pier. The entrance is only a few blocks from the coffee shop. It's a good place to feel like you're part of something bigger than yourself, and, at the same time, a place that doesn't require you to make small talk. The pier is welcoming to pedestrians, sunbathers, dogs, families—lonely poets. I live on the Upper East Side, the most pretentious and heterosexual neighborhood in Manhattan. As a single gay man, I spend my days dodging strollers and watching white women pout behind silent, distant men. Although the West Village is a hike from the Upper East Side, the promise of hairy shirtless men always makes the trek worthwhile.

I'd been reading Brad Gooch's biography of Frank O'Hara, *City Poet*, and was dizzy with the literary history of New York. (I read several chapters sitting on the grass of the pier.) Maybe it's silly, but I wandered around thinking about the places O'Hara had hung out. I'd been reading O'Hara's poems for years, but I had never read the biography. I was also discovering the work of Joe Brainard, his stunning collages and honest, quirky writing. Though the writing was over thirty years old, it felt fresher and more alive than most of the new poetry I'd been reading. It was poetry written as if one's life depended on it. I was drawn to how both Brainard and O'Hara were connected to New York City, to their obsessions, and to some kernel of complicated joy. I was thinking about their ability to make leaps and to manipulate white space (those exclamation points!). I was also drawn to how their writing is present in the action of the moment. The work *is* the happening, not *about* the happening. In the spirit of Brainard, I had been attempting some mediocre collages and had been thinking about the process of the visual artist (about which I know very little). It's not unusual to hear how lonely writing can be, how solitary. Part of the reason I was writing in the coffee shop was to rebel against that notion. I wanted a quiet community to be present while I worked. I thought about the painters I see from time to time standing behind their easels on crowded sidewalks. Could poetry, which relies on the image, be enacted in such a visual sense? Could I write what was happening right in front of me? Could it be more than the present moment recollected at a later time? I also wanted to see if I could write about joy.

One Saturday afternoon, I took my notebook (easel?) down to the pier. I indulged myself by allowing one entire page per section. I wasn't sure what I was writing. I didn't know if they were fragments that would become a larger poem, notes that wouldn't turn in to anything, or the beginnings of several individual poems. I would literally flip a page, write what I saw, then stop. Flip a page, write, stop. I did this over and over for about an hour. I tried to think: What is the most honest, specific thing I can say? What's really there, instead of what I think is there? I put my notebook away. A few days later I started looking through the notebook, and I found a kind of openness in the pieces that I had written. I also found a unifying tone and energy. Most of the poems in my first book were narrative and wrapped up their ideas in a definite way: *This is what happened, and this is how you should feel about it*. With "Christopher Street Pier (Summer)" and other poems in my second manuscript, I was more interested in saying: *This is what happened; do with it what you will*.

The poem was arranged quickly. I left the sections in the order in which I had written them. It felt right in the spirit of the poem: an accurate representation of my experience, the present moment happening in the language. I omitted some sections that weren't pulling their weight or that were doing the same work another section was doing better. I kept the spacing, line breaks, and punctuation that I used while drafting the poem. I tightened a few lines where it wasn't very clear what I was talking about, or where the poet seemed to get too much in the way of the poem. Visually I liked that the poem was spaced out on the page, much like the way the people were clumped together on the pier.

"Christopher Street Pier (Summer)" was a breakthrough poem for me. It helped me understand the way to get a visual, grounded experience on the page in spare, open language. Even though my friend never came back to our friendship, and the elusive man moved in with his boyfriend, writing "Christopher Street Pier (Summer)" helped me figure out how to write a poem that's as fragmented as the way I think, but, at the same time, a poem that does not sacrifice clarity.

Blood

1

Pen filled with ink dark
as the rowanberry,
curious rambler on paper

white as the moon. I've
weathered three hundred
seasons, sun, storm and snow.

Spare in pocket, rich in
the winding of time.
Poemed war, peace, love,

hunger, good bread of this
earth. Why then ache
for a small barefoot boy,

blond hair roughed by
the wind, traipsing
the road to that bridge?

2

Barefoot children sing
out of joy as they scoot
to the bank, whomp stones

from cobbles into the brimming
river, move on to spot freight-
cars creaking up over the hill.

The smallest bloodies his
foot on the bridge. Leaves
friends and cousins, limps

back, skirting houses with fine
carved doors, wild flowers
linking hedges and gardens.

Stops by a wagon bursting
with millet, barley, potatoes,
cabbage, brown eggs, sweetest

blueberries, now to be bartered
for cloth, candles, tools,
holy pictures and tea at his

grandfather's store. The farmer
tends to his foot, shoulders
him onto the thick-necked horse.

Nearby soldiers chat up his mother,
her sisters, jaunty in caps
like the one his father, star

of the Jesuit school, soldier,
lumberjack, dizzy with dreams,
left behind on the way to his

family in the New World. Where
he would prosper, send for
his wife, then with child. Year

by year, on tick, linens,
silverware bearing their name,
laced-collared frocks filled

the room he slept in with
his mother. Soon they would
leave for the port in the farmer's

great wagon. Staring back
at the grandfather, aunts,
uncle, cousins, friends that

he loved. It was good he
was too young to know he was
leaving them all, forever.

3

Blackbird on an eave trough
sings to a boy no longer
barefoot, taking on the language,

landscape of his new place.
Hopping through crisp copper
leaves along the gutters to

the third-floor flat they lodged
in with his father's kin,
who scorned the country girl,

his mother, homesick, wearied
after long hours in a sweatshop
to pay back for linens, silver,

lace stowed in an ocean trunk.
Times, out with his father
at the park, watched him stride off

on his secret missions, silence
meriting a box of Cracker Jacks
on the way home. Soon they had

a lodging of their own, in-a-door bed
for them, sofa for him. Squinting
in the dark he tried to see the

grandfather who'd died in the old country.
Made up stories from vague yesterdays.
Running with his gang, climbing

forbidden structures, aiming
stones from slingshots at back-
alley doors. Doing errands

for the neighbors, taking every
penny home. He had a sister now
and times were hard. They packed up,

wandering state to state, finding
odd jobs. After the market crash
they went back to the city,

and were well set. He had his
own room now, mastered sports,
read his first poem, scribbled

lines exalting the new rug,
sang art songs, arias at school,
for ladies' meetings, Easter Service

in the local church. News sent
his mother to implore her in-laws,
friends to sponsor those she loved,

to help them to the safety of
this shore. They turned away.
Sun fired the lake, fierce colors

of autumn fret-working leaves of
trees he'd shinned up when a boy.
Now Germany was on the march,

rumor echoed beyond winter's strip-
down, bones of branches left
with empty nests. Then Pearl Harbor,

and the struggle had begun. One night
his father woke him with another
secret: word had come his mother's

family had perished. He must never
mention that cursed land again.
As his father spoke he saw them,

cousins, uncle, aunts, friends,
force-marched by the houses with
carved doors, wild flowers joining

hedges, gardens, to the bridge. Shoved
in the freight cars he had waved on
with his chums, hauled a few stops

down the line to death. All night
he heard his mother's agonizing cries.
Next day he signed up, packed his

Leaves of Grass, and went to war.

On "Blood"

"Blood" is the sole truly autobiographical piece I've done and deals with crucial events in my life. Its source is the clear memory of bloodying my foot, when not quite four and playing with friends in Kolo, Poland, and, another memory of the day from almost sixteen years later when my father informed me that my mother's family had perished in their occupied land. The linkage in my imagination came swiftly, and the writing of "Blood" was the result. It too came swiftly, its formal structure, tercets throughout, and unforced diction meant to suggest the calm progression of typical American youth suddenly erupted. The one technical aspect, and a quite consciously introduced element, are the few lyrical passages meant to deepen the flow and emphasize important moments in the progression. Ever since the poem came, I've felt unburdened of the kind of pain felt, I'd imagine by many poets, at least the kind I admire: the need to deal with, and thus perhaps put to rest, the hardest of life's blows.

Mary Swander

Hot Pads, Cold Pads

Hot pads, cold pads,
lift the lid off the stove pads,
squeeze cloth between fingers and pots.
We are what we're not, but do we always need
a go-between—a piece of yarn in hand to stay the burn?

Is that the rubric, the fabric of being born bare-skinned?
Too tender, how did we lose our cover?

The cat, the coon, possum and fox
Slink through the night over brambles and rocks.
Tough paws, they love rough bark and roads.

What scares us?
The roaster, the toaster, the whistling kettle,
The glow of the oven rack, char of skin on wood or pan.
We bend low over flames and

as long as we have tongues and lips to smack,
as long as our stomachs churn and that mad howl
stays clamped in our throats,

we'll use the mitt, we'll take the glove,
and muddle flesh toward mouth.

My kitchen is the same, the clock, the crock, the waves
of heat rising toward your face.
But, love, I am not made of metal,
Let me feel your palm, alone,
Unadorned, pressing down and down.

On the Writing of "Hot Pads, Cold Pads"

The sparks for poems often come to us in odd ways. "Hot Pads, Cold Pads" had a strange beginning.

Jane Smiley was one of my colleagues at Iowa State University when she published her Pulitzer Prize-winning *A Thousand Acres*. We both taught in the creative writing program, part of a large English department. The mailroom was housed in a dark, windowless room lined with a solid wall of wooden mailboxes, one on top of the other. *Names Are under Boxes* the sign read, but it didn't prevent the inevitable confusion of students and secretaries misfiling mail in the box above or below the proper slot.

Jane Smiley's mailbox was directly above mine. Often we ran into each other, pulling memo after memo from our slots, or pitching notices and advertisements into the wastepaper basket. These were the days before e-mail and voice mail, so those snail mailboxes were all-important. Often, I received Jane's mail and vice versa. Mostly, our mail was identical. A form to get your new key to the building. A form to fill out about your consulting activities. A form to report the number of hours you had put in at the university during the past week.

But with *A Thousand Acres* came thousands of letters addressed to Jane Smiley at Iowa State University. When the novel hit the bookstores her mailbox blossomed with fan letters—letters from sincere readers who had enjoyed the Iowa farm story (based on *King Lear*) of a patriarch who lost his farm and his daughters through his own madness. Many of the letters went something like this:

Dear Jane Smiley,

Thank you for writing your brilliant book A Thousand Acres. *Larry Cook could have been my father. You truly depicted the pain of families.*

Then one spring afternoon, Jane was notified that she had won the Pulitzer Prize. The department was abuzz with excitement: people running down the hall and into Jane's office, phones ringing, classes cancelled. That night the English department threw an impromptu party. I ran into the hospital gift shop around the corner from my house and bought a single rose in a vase to present to Jane.

142

The next morning Jane's mailbox began to swell with letters asking her to write magazine articles, to sign copies of her books, to come to universities to give readings, to grant interviews to newspapers and magazines around the world. Jane sorted through these, answered some of them, and let others pile up on the floor of her office. And pile up they did. Day after day, more mail came flooding in. Soon her pigeonhole was crammed full of mail, and some days I would receive her junk mail in my box below hers.

But it was the letter from the Queen of England that finally caught my attention. The letter from the Queen came in an elegant envelope that was stuck—half in and half out—of Jane's box along with all her other fan mail.

I stood at my box that day and sorted through my junk mail—and some of Jane's. "Wow, wouldn't it be neat to have just one piece of fan mail?" I thought.

The next day it arrived. A small package in a brown padded envelope. "What's this?" I wondered and opened the envelope right there in the mail-room for fear it might explode. Among my many junk memos had been one warning not to open any packages from unknown senders. So, I thought, if this package blows up, at least I won't be alone in my office.

A tidy wrapping of tissue paper held two hand-knitted lime-green potholders. The handwriting of an elderly woman told me how much she had enjoyed my gardening book. She had knit these potholders just for me in response to my work.

Ah . . . the Queen of England couldn't have said it better. I took those potholders home and hung them up on the wall in my kitchen. I used them day in and day out as I cooked meals for myself, for my friends, and lovers. One day I sat down at the kitchen table and wrote "Hot Pads, Cold Pads" quite quickly without a lot of revision—unusual for me. In this poem, the re-vision was an emotional leap in my head, one of laughing at myself and fi-nally appreciating a precious object that had simply come to me in the mail—out of nowhere.

Sue Ellen Thompson

Fishing on the Merrimack,
My Father Sees a B-24

Dozing and drifting slowly toward Boscawen
in his battered ten-foot Alumicraft,
he hears the distant rumble of the Flying Boxcar
he and his crew named "Sack

Time Sal" for the hours of blissful rest
they coveted. They flew her over
Sicily and bombed the German base at Trieste
before bailing out 50 years ago.

Now the blunt nose and twin tail
stabilizers emerge from a low-hanging cloud,
its slow propellers pummeling the air.
Following the river from the air show south,

it labors in the shadow of the shadow cast
over my father in his frail craft.

Prisoner of War

He pried loose boards from the walls and floor
to burn in the barracks stove when the chips of coal
ran out. His only clothing was the uniform
he was shot down in, and the Baltic cold

was unrelenting. They killed his bombardier
when, without thinking, he ran out
to catch a fly ball and hit the wire.
The day they expanded the prison compound

to make room for newcomers, my father saw
several yards of untrampled earth to the south.
He tore out handfuls of fresh, raw
onion grass and stuffed it in his mouth.

Doing swell, his letters to my mother said.
Don't worry your pretty little head.

From Sunday Supplement to Sonnet Sequence: A Poet's Gift to Herself

After twenty years of writing query letters, entering contests, and begging friends to ask their editors to look at my work, I was finally in the enviable position of having a completed manuscript and a press eager to publish it. But when I sent my editor at Autumn House Press the manuscript for my fourth book—consisting only of the poems that had survived my own arduous and self-critical selection process—he sent almost half of them back. "I don't want you to freak out," he warned me in a phone call the day before the package arrived, "but I don't think you're there yet." Where, exactly, was "there," and how was I supposed to reach it in ten months—the deadline for inclusion in his 2006 publication schedule?

I am a slow writer, an obsessive reviser, and consider it a good year when I have ten to twelve finished poems. Now, suddenly, I had to come up with more than thirty. Revisiting the poems that I'd left out of the manuscript the first time around—hoping to discover that I had been too harsh in judging them—proved discouraging: Knowing that my editor was holding me to such a high standard made me even less likely to find them worthy.

But he had also provided me with a hint as to how I might proceed. Because the bulk of the poems in that early version of *The Golden Hour* concerned my mother's illness and death and what I had observed during that final period in my parents' marriage, my editor wanted to know more. "Your parents were married for almost sixty years," he pointed out. "Surely there was more to their relationship than what took place during those last seventeen weeks."

To refresh my memory of the family history, I turned to a prose piece I had written in 1995 for *Northeast*, the Sunday magazine section of the *Hartford Courant*. Titled "Diary of Stalag Luft 1," it chronicled my father's World War II experiences, from his days as a young B-24 pilot training in Texas to the bombing runs he made from Grottaglie, in the "heel" of southern Italy, over German air bases in northern Italy and Yugoslavia. It told the story of how he'd been shot down on January 31, 1944, over Aviano, Italy, where he had managed to release his bombs on one of the largest German fighter bases before bailing out and being taken prisoner. Rereading the article brought back a great deal about my father and the early days of my parents' marriage.

At the very end of the *Northeast* article, I described a day more than four decades later, after my father had retired to a farm in New Hampshire:

In 1984, my father took his battered 11-foot Alumicraft out on the Merrimack River one day to fish for bass. Drowsing in the late afternoon sun, his line snagging the current as the boat drifted toward Boscawen, he was roused by a distant rumbling. Although 45 years had passed, he recognized it immediately as belonging to a B-24. Soon he could distinguish the blunt nose, narrow fuselage, and twin tail stabilizers, and the sound of four propellers pummeling the air was unmistakable. On its way home from a show at Pease Air Force Base, the plane flew low, following the course of the river and casting its huge shadow over my father in his much smaller craft.

Something about the last half of that final sentence—perhaps it was the assonance in *casting*, *shadow*, and *craft*—struck me as having poetic potential. Within minutes, I had come up with the following couplet: "It labors in the shadow of the shadow cast/ over my father in his frail craft." I liked the way repeating "the shadow" reinforced the enormous influence that the war and his two-and-a-half years as a POW had had on my father's life.

A sonnet rushed in to fill the void that formed behind this couplet, much of its language drawn directly from that prose paragraph: the drowsing and

drifting toward Boscawen, the "battered 11-foot Alumicraft" (which I short-
ened by a foot for rhythmic purposes), the "blunt nose" and "twin tail stabiliz-
ers," and the "propellers pummeling the air." I also included details from
elsewhere in the article: the "Flying Boxcar," synonymous with the B-24;
"Sack Time Sal," the name that my father and his crew had given their plane;
and details about their final bombing run, although I moved the target fifty
miles southeast to Trieste—this time to suit the demands of the rhyme
scheme. Within a day or two, I had a finished Shakespearean sonnet that em-
ployed off rhyme but otherwise adhered to tradition. It satisfied me in a way
that many of my more hard-won and labored-over poems had not, perhaps
because I was reaping a second reward for the effort I had put into the prose
piece ten years earlier. Perhaps, also, because I realized that I had enough ma-
terial in that article to produce a few more sonnets like it.

Here is another example of two prose passages, both concerning my
father's POW experience, that were easily fitted together as a sonnet:

The winter of 1944-45 was the worst Northern Europe had expe-
rienced in decades. The cold was particularly bitter in Barth, which
was at about the same latitude as Canada's Hudson Bay. Life as a
kriegsgefangen—the prisoners referred to themselves as "kriegies"—
quickly assumed a harsh routine as they struggled to stay warm by
burning the bricks of compressed coal dust that camp officials al-
lotted them. When these ran out, they would often pry loose
boards from the walls or floor of the poorly constructed barracks
and burn them as well. Their only clothing was what they were
wearing when they were taken prisoner, although my father re-
members sleeping in a heavy GI overcoat that was issued later by
the Red Cross. He still remembers the day the prison compound
was expanded to accommodate its burgeoning population and he
was allowed to walk on a previously untrampled piece of ground.
Almost immediately, he fell to his knees and started pulling up
handfuls of lush green onion grass, which he used that night to
flavor his daily ration of potato soup.

This time it was a particular phrase—"lush green onion grass"—that struck
me as the starting point for a poem. But the closing couplet did not come to
me in a flash; on the contrary, I wrote the three quatrains without having any
idea how the sonnet would end. Then my editor's admonition to write more
about my parents' marriage sent me back to a small bundle of letters that had
survived from my father's years as a POW. It was in one of these that I
found the words for the missing couplet: "Doing swell. Don't worry your
pretty little head."

As a sometime teacher and workshop leader, I have often shown my students how Edward Thomas, the British poet who was Robert Frost's close friend when the two were neighbors in England before World War I, had plundered a long prose passage in one of his own travel books, *The Icknield Way,* to write "Rain," one of his most moving poems. Perhaps because I don't write prose that often, it never occurred to me that I might do the same. In the end, "Diary of Stalag Luft 1" and my parents' wartime correspondence yielded more than a dozen sonnets within a couple of months and prompted the writing of two dozen more. By the time I resubmitted *The Golden Hour* for publication at the end of 2005, the manuscript included thirty-two Shakespearean sonnets, four of which were eventually read by Garrison Keillor on *The Writer's Almanac* and another of which was the subject of Ted Kooser's nationally syndicated newspaper column, "American Life in Poetry." More important, I had learned that the seeds for some of my best poems had already been planted. I had only to remember where.

Natasha Trethewey

Myth

I was asleep while you were dying.
It's as if you slipped through some rift, a hollow
I make between my slumber and my waking,

the Erebus I keep you in, still trying
not to let go. You'll be dead again tomorrow,
but in dreams you live. So I try taking

you back into morning. Sleep-heavy, turning,
my eyes open, I find you do not follow.
Again and again, this constant forsaking.

∾

Again and again, this constant forsaking:
my eyes open, I find you do not follow.
You back into morning, sleep-heavy, turning.

But in dreams you live. So I try taking,
not to let go. You'll be dead again tomorrow.
The Erebus I keep you in—still, trying—

I make between my slumber and my waking.
It's as if you slipped through some rift, a hollow.
I was asleep while you were dying.

MYTHMAKING

As promised, I am going to try to put down as much as I can about the writing of my poem "Myth." There are things I remember, and many that I don't. I know that notes for this poem first appeared in my journal in 2001. I was at Harvard on a Bunting Fellowship. When I had my entrance interview/discussion with the director of the fellowship program, she told me that nothing official was expected of me—no progress report, no finished or nearly finished project—to account for how I spent my time. She then told me that many fellows had used their Bunting year to rest; that one of them had used her time to grieve the death of her father, whom she'd never had time to grieve before this glorious year of freedom from professional responsibilities.

I know that this stuck with me as I left her office and walked back down Garden Street toward my lovely rooms near Harvard Square. I must have been thinking about my own grieving process and to what extent I had grieved my mother's death almost twenty years earlier. I was approaching that anniversary, and I had never been able to write well about her death. I had never visited a therapist to discuss my loss.

I know too that I was looking ahead to my fortieth birthday in 2006. I always measure my time in increments that are symbolic to me; when I was approaching twenty-six, I kept thinking about how that was how old my mother was when I was first aware of her age. (We had a birthday party for her and I had made a cake in the shape of a watermelon half. No candles— black seeds marked her twenty-six years.) Later I was fixated on my Jesus year, my thirty-third year, and how my name means "Christmas child." I thought I wouldn't survive that year because I am such a literalist. I was thinking death and crucifixion when I should have been thinking figuratively; I should have been thinking resurrection. Now, I was thinking about forty— the last age my mother ever was. I think this is why I started writing some poems that dealt with her death and my grief. I was approaching her age and the twenty-year anniversary of her death at the same time. And I had just gotten a job offer from Emory University, and I would be moving back to the geography of my past and my great loss.

So, with all this swirling around in my conscious and subconscious mind, I wrote some things down in my journal. A list of words appeared on a Post-it note in my journal, like this:

fossil
eros/erosion
errand/errant
ergo   aphasia
erebus   etymology

152

permanence
gesture   apostasy
supplication intaglio

Then there were a few more pages of Post-its, and on the fourth one I had written:

I was asleep while you were dying. It was as if
you slipped through
the rift between my
slumber &   (in my consciousness—
into   my waking—the un)
the erebus I make now
with my grief. Some
mornings arrive

And on the next page:

with visions of you
as in the myth I try
to see,
open my eyes in
waking and you do
not follow.
Over and over I send
you back.

It seems that I had sketched most of the poem's thinking in those few rough lines. I know that from here I typed a draft into my computer. I printed what I'd typed and put it in a drawer, an unfinished fragment.

I know that I forgot about this unfinished, unsuccessful poem for a long time. In the meantime, I was writing other poems in an elegiac mood and putting them away in drawers too. Some of their first drafts are also in that same notebook. They began to emerge from my drawer as editors solicited poems from me. I am a slow writer, and I would always say I didn't have anything. But I began to feel that I should submit something for their consideration lest I damage my relationships with folks who believed in my poems. So I started looking back in those drawers. I don't know exactly when I read the draft of "Myth" again, but I think it was around 2003. I could see it anew then, and I quickly completed a draft that I didn't think was too bad. This draft was only a version of the first half of the poem. Much of this is a blur now, but I do know that I then noticed a few words that rhymed; so, I went through the draft and made the changes that would allow the tercets to have a blend of slant and exact rhyme: dying waking, trying taking, turning forsaking, hollow, tomorrow, follow.

I don't know when it occurred to me that the poem could work as a palindrome. I do know that I tend to read my line endings to get a sense of the integrity of a line, and I can imagine that I tested the poem's worth by reading it backwards, line by line. Or maybe that isn't what happened at all. Maybe I went back to thinking about the myth of Orpheus and Eurydice and how my dreams of my mother echoed the action of the myth. I had thought about the myth originally, after all. So perhaps I began to think about that journey into sleep, into dream, as similar to Orpheus's journey into the underworld. An erebus is a kind of otherworldly liminal space, and I had written that word d in an early list of words whose sounds (and meanings) had attracted me. I know that when I began thinking about the poem's added formal elements that I had to rethink and change some words; for example, I needed the state of slumber, which is different from sleep in that slumber is the light sleep before the REM sleep of dream. I also had to rewrite the lines that include the phrase "sleep-heavy, turning, my eyes open" so that I could create an image that would suggest Orpheus's turning and looking as Eurydice vanishes; that would equate with my tossing and turning awake and opening my eyes at the point of my mother's disappearance back into the liminal erebus, the space of that other world of dream where she still exists, alive but out of reach.

Brian Turner

At the Farmer's Market in Eugene

Behind the storefront glass, a television set
broadcasts a familiar scene: a woman with fists
knuckling white, her mouth shocked open
as if wailing, or at the dry end of wailing,
though no one hears it, no one notices
her face framed in a black abaya, eyes
lined in charcoal, the color of the shadows
trailing behind us as we pass by, arms
filled with bags of cauliflower, ossified heads.

In the farmer's market, each stall overflows
with artichoke hearts, tangelos, mandarin oranges.
Lady finger grapes slip from the palms of the dead,
whose hands fill the stacked boxes, among spears
of asparagus, the missing limbs of the wounded, pickled
radishes and ketchup jars shelved like pints of blood
left open behind the vendors. And the woman

in the television, she stares at the incomprehensible
sunflowers, honey from Volcano Island, skins
of avocados hardening into hand grenades.
She sees how veterans kiss their wives
with the taste of bullets on their tongues,
as sparrows and finches sing in the birches

above the children, a choir for the dead
who have traveled so far to be here among us.
Here where the fountain shoots a crude and oily stream
for the bright coins of lovers who make their wishes
and don't look back. No one notices the woman
in the television, the wreckage surrounding her,
the smoldering and twisted metal, though if,

if I just stopped for a moment, here in front of her,
I might feel the heat blowing past her and into the street,
I might smell what no one should ever smell,
holding her with my arms to shield her
from the wild trajectories of bullets, the crackling
applause of white phosphorous as it bursts
into fireworks over the local football game.

And the old man with the saxophone
might put down his horn, as dazed shoppers
exit the storefronts, their eardrums ringing,
everything they touch given the fingerprint
of blood, an art the small children duplicate
on the sidewalks, where I hold this woman
and guide her to the nearby grass, easing her
down under the contrails of fighter jets
banking in the curve of another bombing run,
as I whisper words that mean nothing to her,
my face a dark shadow eclipsing the sun,
my hair on fire with it, the words in my mouth
falling around her like spent shell casings of brass,
while someone yells nearby for people to run
back inside, *Get t-shirts, tampons—anything*
to stop the bleeding.

Brian Turner

In a Country at War

I'm listening to Brad Mehldau's *Exit Music (For a Film)*. It seems well suited to melancholy. Strings resonate within the piano, building in arpeggios. The tips of drumsticks discover how rain might fall in the cymbal's hammered brass. And behind it all, a string bass, a sound of wood and air. It's a black-and-white film, I think, one with long tracking shots and one that explores a psychological interior through visual metaphors expressed by buildings, streets, the curving ribs of umbrellas, the lights of a city smeared in rain. Or maybe it's snowing. Leaves spiral colorlessly down in autumn. It is January, and the lovers will never see each other again. It is Prague, or the waterfront in Chicago. Someone, somewhere, has died.

I feel like I'm stealing the noir of this music. Cheapening it with the lonely clichés in my head. In fact, this is not a black-and-white film and—for the first time in months—winter feels erased by the sun. I'm in California and the midday light casts a crosshatching of shadows through the enormous crowns of palm trees, each frond and its shadow swaying in a slight breeze I imagine only hours ago to have lifted an albatross flying out over the Pacific Ocean.

From where I now sit, it's a three-hour drive to the ocean—if you push the accelerator some—and it's also been nearly three-and-a-half years since my desert boots walked through the streets of the Iraqi northern city of Mosul. I'm drinking a mocha topped with whipped cream. If I were to MapQuest where I am now, the closest I might get would be the intersection of Via La Plata and Blackstone Avenues. It wouldn't map the comfortably cushioned chair where I'm sitting, nor the pounds I've gained since I last wore my combat fatigues.

The war feels distant and removed from this place. And yet, somehow, this music, voiced in piano and bass and drums, this *Exit Music (For a Film),* begins to strip away some of the studio backdrop, bringing the world more clearly into focus. And when I am attentive to its visuals, I begin to discover much more than I saw at first glance: The avocados at the farmer's market become hand grenades; heirloom tomatoes become pints of blood, sealed with green and twisting stems; the shoppers leaving the stalls at the market cross the street and pass by me, smiling and talking to one another, answering their cell phones and morphing into 911 operators receiving medevac requests from a war zone, calls they can't hear, losing the language in static and apologizing to the callers by saying, "I'm so sorry; I can't hear you; please try again." These two worlds begin to fuse, one into the other. And I've been thinking about this for quite some time now.

157

I took an artist's sketchpad (a 9-by 12-inch Strathmore sketchbook, to be exact) over to Von's supermarket a couple of weeks back, my purpose being to scout out language, images, words in their raw form, waiting for what I might make of them. The mercurial and the mundane. I wrote them down. Grocery clerks walked by and gave me that you're-one-of-those-crazy-people looks. But I didn't care. I wrote lists of brand names: Mr. Clean, All, Cheer, Easy-Off, Shout, and Kaboom! I found scents and oils promising: Hawaiian Breezes, Blue Tranquility, Meadows & Rain. Some of this became part of the following stanza (lines I later cut because the singing of them was getting in the way of the song itself):

> . . . And the woman in the television,
> she just stares at it all, the stalks of sunflowers, honey
> imported from Volcano Island, the skins of avocados
> hardened into hand grenades. She's watched
> the freight trucks pulling into the loading bays
> of America, long past midnight, their engines
> idling in exhaust the way ships rocked
> side by side on the shores of Ilium—
> heavy with Lysol, Kaboom, and Shout.
> She's seen the stockboys lifting crate after crate
> of Arm & Hammer, Easy-Off, Mr. Clean.
> They bring air fresheners in scents
> of *citrus & light, clean linen, blushing apple*
> and *chamomile*. Glade scented oils promising
> *Hawaiian breezes, meadows & rain*.
> They bring seven shelves of hair products—
> gels, moisturizers, sprays and conditioners,
> spiking glue, styling paste, sculpting wax.

Still, as I walked through the produce section and the aisles of cleaning products, greeting cards, wine and beer—an obsession began. As one day passed into another, I had the title of this poem (which was originally "Saturday Market") reminding me that below the level of my conscious thought, work was underway. A poem was in the making, but I needed a way in. I needed a doorway.

So I read. And while reading James Riverbend's *Baghdad Burning II: More Girl Blog from Iraq (Women Writing the Middle East)* (2006), which is available from the Feminist Press, I found a doorway into my own poem. Here are the sentences that did it: "Sometimes I'll be watching the news and the volume will be really low. The scene will be of a man, woman, or child, wailing in front of a camera; crying at the fate of a body lying bloodily, stiffly on the ground—a demolished building in the background. . . ." It immediately reminded me of standing in an airport, engulfed in the noise, while television monitors played news footage from the war in Iraq; a woman on the screen was wailing, her voice drowned out by intercoms and cell phone talkers and the general audio blur created by travelers in the aggregate.

So I create an electronics store across the street from the farmer's market. I unplug the television I watched in the Dallas International Airport terminal and place it so that the Iraqi woman in the black abaya might witness this seemingly quiet moment in Fresno. I take out my sketchbook and begin to sketch the world of this poem, stanza by stanza. Brad Mehldau accompanies me on piano. The date palms sway above—so real I begin to confuse where this world ends and the next one begins.

When I e-mail these stanzas to my friend the poet Ilyse Kusnetz, she says, "You are getting where you need to go, and, remember: lyricism will carry the grammar." And of course she's right. I'm writing down the lists. I'm sketching the grenades as their bodies turn explosive. I'm wondering where I am in the music. What do I share with this woman who has come so far from her home, a woman who brings me a lesson of war I may or may not learn, depending on how hard I listen for what she might have to teach me?

And maybe this has been my problem all along. I'm confused by this world because I'm not really listening to what it wants to say. I keep imposing myself upon it. I keep talking and talking. Another friend, the poet and editor April Ossmann, says that I'm bogging the poem down, that I'm delaying the action. So, I make a decision. Focus the camera. Listen to the music. Let Brad Mehldau play the piano, and let the Iraqi woman step out of the screen to walk among us here in California, here at the farmer's market.

A '71 Impala backfires and the Iraqi woman doesn't flinch. There are bullets hissing through the air. There are people drinking upside-down caramel macchiatos. Children finger-paint the sidewalk in blood. And the woman has come here to die. And I don't understand any of it. And when she looks up at me, a man speaking what words I can for the dying, her very look smolders and burns me to the core. My words fall like spent shells. My hair catches fire.

Lee Upton

The Weak Already Inherited

Pussy willows budded warheads this year—
that was the forsythia's job.
Butterflies advanced without mercy.
That cup of tea swallowed the entire
National Convention of Broadcasters.
Among the newborns are the snipers
most likely to pick us off.
The prawns set a precedent,
torching twice as many cars as last month.
Remember the egg that broke into the deli
to revenge its mother?
It never could be restrained.
Maybe the water buffalo *like*
being overturned by the scallops—
has anyone thought of that?
Those three toothpicks sure took out
their frustrations on the submarine.
That rainbow made quick work
of muscling in on the lucrative drug trade.
Feathers bashed in a gate.
Weird about the oysters renting that outsized chalet
in Switzerland

just to manipulate worldwide oil prices.
And you.
I hope you have a license
to feed the wolves
to the sheep again.
All my sheep are sore
from herding the question mark.

RESPONSE

"The Weak Already Inherited" grew from one line: "The butterflies advanced without mercy." That line arrived in a draft about the dark wood of Dante. During revisions, the line dropped out and moved into other poems. It fell away each time, not like a prop that was no longer necessary to hold up a house, but like a dead fly. The line was trying to fit in, poor thing, expiring on the window ledge of poem after poem.

At last I did what I should have done all along and isolated and duplicated the line's logic: the vulnerable and powerless create outrageous havoc. Of course, statements about a counterfactual world can go on forever: The meat cleaver doesn't stand a chance now that the cheese isn't alone. A cluster of grapes brained the orchestra. Last night a button made ribbons out of the shark. I hope you have a warrant for those teardrops.

After I began with "The butterflies advanced without mercy," the phrase with the word *forsythia* appeared, at which point I knew there was traction for the poem, given the wonderful aural effects of *forsythia*, a word impossible to say without sounding at least vaguely comical or entertainingly pretentious.

Succeeding lines reoccupy familiar strands of language: "set a precedent," "It never could be restrained," "Has anyone thought of that?" "quick work," "muscling in on the lucrative drug trade," "worldwide oil prices." These are overly familiar phrases, but I confess a fondness for handling such phrases, to the point of working with outright clichés in some of my poems. To the saying, "If it were any closer it would bite you," a poem of mine responds: "You should rise to the occasion, if the occasion weren't so desperate to kick you." To the phrase, "Who died and made you queen?" I couldn't help responding: "Who lived to make you their servant?" It's hard to resist certain sayings— although I've never found a legitimate way to deal with the most horrid saying I grew up with, a saying that would freeze any complaint: "What do you want? A sugar titty?" (Apparently what's being referred to is a rag soaked in sweetened water—something for babies to suck on to keep them from crying. The saying probably worked better than the rag, let me tell you.)

162

As I drafted "The Weak Already Inherited," I wasn't thinking of the drawbacks of writing lines that replicated a central strategy. What drew me forward were the unlikely juxtapositions, which pleased me, as well as the possibility of imagining inverting the order of life on earth. The poem acts as whimsical revenge, breaking from the absurdities of common violence with the absurdities of imagined violence that simply cannot take place.

For over a month "The Weak Already Inherited" ended at the lines, "Weird about the oysters renting that outsized chalet / in Switzerland / just to manipulate worldwide oil prices." Whenever I tried to follow up with other lines, the poem collapsed. Yet I wanted the poem to conclude on a less distant chord, to become less whimsical even if, at heart, the poem respects whimsy. The simple, direct words "And you," once arrived at, led me to the ending. After all, who has ever heard those two words without stiffening in anticipation? And of course the imagination can feed wolves to sheep. At least, it can now. And who isn't herded by the question mark? Then again, the question mark is not only a sign of anxiety but of curiosity, which is the partial antidote to anxiety.

I am fond of Zbigniew Herbert's statement about someone else's poetry: "I don't remember his poems just that they were moist." I remember so much about writing this poem because of the line that made it possible. Through several revisions, "The butterflies advanced without mercy" floated through the poem, landing at different spots. Finally I put the butterflies right after the forsythia—where they would be, in the world of fact, more likely to land. During early drafts the poem was titled "The Meek Shall Inherit." Next it became "The Weak Shall Inherit." Then, in a bid for precision, the title became "The Weak Already Inherited." Only recently did I look up the phrase "The meek shall inherit the earth" in the King James Bible to consider it in context. The rest of the line of the psalm is "and shall delight themselves in the abundance of peace."

G. C. Waldrep

Anniversary

for Peter Streckfus

(1)

The voyage to the anniversary was carpeted with the shed leaves of the peanut tree.

We walked to the anniversary on the legs of the tortoise and the giraffe. We sailed to the anniversary on barques made of India rubber.

The locomotive by which we reached the anniversary ran on a high rail of burnished acetaminophen.

All the bicycle paths led past the anniversary and on into a salubrious regret. Nevertheless we allowed the cyclists to pass our rickshaws, doffing our saffron tams in their various directions.

Flights into and out of the anniversary were much too expensive. The funicular railway and luge runs were options, when the weather was cold enough.

We planned our voyage to the anniversary with utmost care.

Some of us brought husbands, wives, lovers along. Some of us brought children, some dogs. One brought a pet parakeet in a jade cage.

The jungles that lay between us and the anniversary were said to be impenetrable. The deserts that lay between us and the anniversary were reported to be without oases, and inhabited by deadly scorpions and serpents.

The plains that lay between us and the anniversary were dotted with rosebushes whose thorns were said to be haunted. The swamps were whispered to have been drained and replaced by something even more dreadful, nobody knew quite what.

The intercepting mountains were very tall. Our horses stumbled on the rocky paths; the howdahs and elephants tipped crazily. Our chartered buses labored in the hairpin curves.

And always, beneath our feet, the shed leaves of the peanut tree.

(2)

For there to exist an anniversary two preconditions must be met: a Point of Reference, and a Means of Interval. The topography and disposition of any anniversary depends upon these necessary qualia.

In most cases the Point of Reference constitutes an Event, the Means of Interval a Calendar.

Often, along the way to an anniversary, a new Point of Reference—a new Event—is added to memory, that is, adumbrated within the Calendar.

This simply creates another anniversary.

Only rarely does a new Means of Interval interrupt a journey to an anniversary. It is more likely that a new means of transportation will present itself.

As we journeyed toward the anniversary we discussed these things.

The flickering of firelight against the liana at evening. The sirocco. The warm breath of the huskies in the snow.

(3)

During the day, from the backs of the camels and in the subway cars and in the tumbrels pulled by oxen, we studied the protocols of the anniversary.

There was, traditionally, sacrifice, of specie or livelihood. Likewise the superimposition of event upon Event, commemorative.

There would doubtless be certain local variations, oblique embroideries of culture, opportunities for error.

Distracted as we were by the frantic signaling of the castaways we must have missed some important points.

We understood that pilgrimages to the anniversary were often botched in the last possible moment.

We understood that this was serious business.

And yet, looking up into the tangled nests of hummingbirds in the heart of some metropolitan constituency we felt our hearts lighten more than once.

For we perceived that the protocol of the anniversary unfolds inexorably along the journey, just as the journey itself is an essential aspect of that protocol.

We sang songs as we rowed, maintained moments of silence in the elevators.

(4)

There will be some who maintain that the anniversary is arbitrary, even mythical—that the literature of the anniversary is an elaborate hoax:

Either the precipitating Event never happened, or it did but its actual date and significance can no longer be fixed;

or else the Means of Interval is unreliable, owing to the sectarian tendencies of our major religious traditions or perhaps the almost imperceptible errancy of our planet as it caroms through what we think of as space.

A certain degree of concision is unavoidable.

There will be, in the capitals, lecture series to denounce both the idea of the anniversary and the prospect of any journey.

There will be, in the rural districts, anathema pronounced by local shamans on those who either do or do not observe the protocols, the washings, the tithes of mint and cumin, the tying of threads.

It is so easy to lose track of such things.

Over the centuries many guidebooks have been written, even published, providing advice, commentary, maps. When the weather was good, we read these books with interest. When the weather was bad, we fed their pages to our fires.

(5)

Once, while fording a treacherous mountain cataract, it occurred to me that we might have missed the anniversary entirely and moved on, like the cyclists, into regret.

I mentioned this to my remaining companion, who merely laughed.

We had been warned that although the water looked bracing and clear, it contained leeches, and the current was swift and deadly. We had even been taught, by the locals, a charm to murmur, in a singsongy sort of voice, as prophylactic against either the leeches or the current, or perhaps both.

It is with great grief and—yes—regret that I confess to you I no longer recall the words or the melody to that charm.

You will suggest I contact my companion, whose memory might exceed mine. Or that perhaps together we will be able to piece together what we each, individually, have lost.

When we parted, it was a cloudy day. A warm wind from the south stirred the volcanic ash of the plain, flecking his parka and my beard.

Flocks of pelicans wheeled overhead, dark stars in a milky sky.

(6)

There is of course more to say on the subject of sacrifice, also the disposition and relative plenitude of food and lodging along the most-travelled routes;

about the help we received, and the many obstacles that were laid in our paths;

about the shadows cast by those who made the journey, and the prismatic effect of certain cloud formations; about both light and its interruption.

At night, as we slept, we often cried out, dreaming.

And always, underfoot,

> beneath the tires and the snowshoes,
> used as bookmarks,
> encrusted in the fossilized shale,
> clinging to the stiff coats of llamas or the welcome mats of
>   teahouses,
> buried with corpses for good luck,
> encased in pastry,   pounded into papyrus,
> distilled into ink or unguent,
> folded gently into aromatic stews or used as currency
> or else floating on the surface of those waters—

cynosure, unburdening cathexis, prayer to Mnemosyne half-mumbled at the immense amethyst altar of waking as of sleep—

the fact of that laughter. And the shed leaves of the peanut tree.

REVISITING THE ANNIVERSARY: A GHOST STORY

People, poets included, go to poetry for a variety of reasons. Some turn to poetry in the hope that the known world will be taken from them and, through the power of the poet's vision and craft, returned fresh, wondrous, affective. Others turn to poetry not for a repackaging of known experience, but rather for an entirely *new* experience: poetry as a vehicle for exploration or discovery, mystery, revelation even, things we don't know—perhaps *can't* know—outside of poetry.

The best poems perform both functions simultaneously.

Compositional processes are as various as the poems they engender. Some of my poems start with a fragment of language, either something I've overheard or something I've come up with on my own; more rarely, an image. There is this intuitive sense that something is *there,* something more than the words for their own sakes: a possibility, an opening. When I was eight, my parents took me to visit a moonstone mine in rural Virginia. I couldn't tell true moonstone from quartzite until someone showed me how to hold up any planar surface to the light at just the right angle, so that I would catch the telltale iridescence. These bits of generative language are like that: you see, or sense, that flash in the mind's light.

Just as often, though, I simply sit down and start writing, or typing, to see what happens. It's disconcertingly like tuning my inner radio station to the Z frequency just to see what's broadcasting. Sometimes it's static. Sometimes it's noise from the culture. Sometimes I catch a few notes that sound like a song. Sometimes something else—something new—comes through loud and clear.

I don't recall anything special about the day I drafted "Anniversary." The original draft is dated 1/6/07. I was in Ohio and it was raining, a cold, steady rain. I had been immersed in the literature of dada, especially Tristan Tzara, for a class I would be teaching that spring. I had completed two manuscripts the year before and was in the desultory process of revising them. I was not very happy with the poems I had written the previous summer or fall. I vaguely recall I'd heard someone say something about "going to the anniversary"—an anniversary *celebration*, no doubt. I recall thinking, at some point in the days or weeks since I had heard it, that this was a remarkable thing to say.

But on the day I drafted the poem, I simply sat down without much in mind and typed what I typed. I was as surprised as anyone.

After I was done, I tried to imagine what might have prompted the poem, to whom or from what it might be speaking. Somehow my mind, or my muse, settled on a book by a friend, *The Cuckoo* by Peter Streckfus, which I had read several years before. I can't really say why or how "Anniversary" constitutes a response to *The Cuckoo,* although they share a certain episodic periodicity. I wasn't consciously thinking of Peter or his book while I was drafting "Anniversary." I was just typing, at first as a sort of exercise, a joke even, but then, as sometimes happens, the material pushed its way past humor and into stranger territory.

What if the anniversary existed, as a place? Would we want to go there?

When I speak to students about the importance of revision, I often feel like a fraud. The reason for this is that nearly every poem I have ever drafted was composed from start to finish in one sitting. (The "Battery" sequence from my second collection, *Disclamor*, is an exception, but it was designed that way, as an experiment, an exception.) If I am interrupted while writing, that's it. The poem has to take on its full contours during the initial compositional phase. It's easier for me to start a new poem than to re-enter a partial draft after the generative impulse has fled.

My own revision process seems to have two parts. On the one hand, I am an obsessive reviser of diction, line breaks, and stanzation. After I've drafted a poem, there is a period—between several hours and several days—during which it feels mutable, plastic, "wet" like the surface of a fresco. During this period I go through anywhere from three to thirty drafts. If I am working on a word processor, I print out each distinct draft, so that I can see the words on a page. Sometimes I use poster gum to affix successive or competing drafts of a poem to the walls, so that I can gain some visual vantage on what's happening, how the poem is moving.

Within a week, the poem tends to feel done, for better or for worse. Or at least the surface hardens. Again, it's easier for me to start a new poem than to fix a bad one, though I may keep tinkering for several months.

The other part of revision is the act of *re-vision*: of trying to understand just what the poem is trying to do or say or show, and then, perhaps, moving it more effectively toward those goals. Since my process is almost entirely intuitive—I never know where I am going when I start a poem (if I know where I am going, the result is usually prose)—I often have only the foggiest notion of what the poem means once it feels done. Meaning, for me, is something that accrues slowly, gradually, over a period of months or even years.

"Anniversary" went through a number of drafts early on, and then two successive rounds of tweaking: once when it was accepted by *Denver Quarterly* and again after that issue of *DQ* came out. That said, it remains structured pretty much as in the original draft. The changes mostly had to do with fine-tuning the music, especially in the last two sections.

As for what the poem might mean?

I think it means we live surprising lives, often in surprising ways.

Some days I think it is, in the end, a ghost story. (But aren't they all?)

Lucian Blaga writes, "Our duty, when faced by a true mystery, is not to explain it, but to deepen it, to transform it into a greater mystery." Charles Simic adds, "The world is beautiful but not sayable. That's why we need art."

Beloved

Romania, 1989

She cradles the rag-swathed, 40-watt bulb
Like a hand-painted egg in woolen gloves
With holes scissored at forefinger and thumb
For turning pages in the icy nook.
The library looms beyond gritty drifts,
Past blood-soaked slats and the empty, grease-glossed
Hooks beckoning from butcher shop windows.

Last week she began reading *Ethan Frome*,
A donated copy—some Fulbright prof's—
And felt that New England snowscape her own,
But the volume's vanished between visits.
She hopes Ethan chose love over duty.
Still, she can't bring herself to steal a book;
Ceauşescu won't be shot until Christmas.
She scours shelves for American novels—
Overhead bulbs fizzled out years ago—
Then finds the harrowing tale of a slave
That makes her bulb seem to surge with power
Hour after hour in the cold cubicle.
(A decade later she'll meet the author.)
Sixteen now, she can't anticipate much,
Except to be loved as she loves these books.
                    for Mihaela

THE ECCENTRIC DISCIPLINE

During the past decade or so, I've been writing, often but not always, sometimes without intention, syllabic verse. I don't count syllables as I draft a poem, but have found that certain cadences, those of decasyllabic lines or their variation—alternating lines of thirteen and seven syllables, for example—insist themselves as the poem takes shape. "There are those who say that you cannot hear syllabics," Eric Pankey has stated, "that as a form it is only an obstacle for the writer. But I believe that we can train our ears to listen for the most subtle patterns in the language, syllabics being only one such pattern." For a long time I have written by ear, allowing the sounds of words to suggest other words as the poem progresses, trusting "the sound of sense," as Robert Frost called it. Such chiming effects help to keep the entire poem in the foreground, each word snug in its line, each equally important. "A poem is not a poem," John Logan insisted, "unless it has an essential surface to it which is musical in character." Rhyming all along the lines while the lines themselves remain taut yet shapely creates a tension that may suit the emotional content of my work. The fluidity of the diction ripples across linear paths like water winding through a creek bed. Each line surprises, hurtling forward or slowing to gather more force or shifting direction, yet seems the inevitable result of all preceding lines. "As systems go, syllabic verse has little to recommend it," writes Brad Leithauser, "except for one puzzling thing: It works. With some frequency, the eccentric discipline it imposes seems to push everyday utterance into memorability."

"Beloved" was written in the fall of 2005 on the island of Malta, where I was enjoying a five-week residency fellowship at the St. James Centre for Creativity. I wrote each day, starting in early morning, then ambled the waterfront promenade for several hours in late afternoon, a walk that became part of the process of revision. I carried the poem with me, and stopped often to add a line, delete several, or strike one word and substitute another; then stopped again to replace the stricken word. I had made several decisions, all arbitrary, regarding my writing before arriving on Malta: I would work every day, almost all day; I would move forward every other day with a new poem rather than keep deepening into one poem, as was my habit (otherwise I might work on only one poem the entire residency); I would keep the poems short; and I would avoid syllabic scaffolding. I came home with fourteen new poems, all short, all but two strictly decasyllabic. Go figure.

My wife, Mihaela, accompanied me to Malta. She had grown up in Romania, not leaving until 1996 when she was twenty-four, seven years after the violent revolution that ended with the execution by improvised firing squad of dictator Nicolae Ceaușescu and his wife, Elena, on Christmas Day, 1989.

Her stories of life under communism were fascinating and horrifying, and I felt strongly that they should remain hers, to be told in her own poems, in her own style. Yet in writing this love poem, I filched, with permission, one detail from that life: she had to bring her own light bulb to the library in order to read there. All other details in the poem are imagined, except for the reference to the death of Ceauşescu and the fact that Mihaela and I would have dinner with Toni Morrison in 2001. The title is borrowed, of course, from the novel of the same name by Ms. Morrison, but might be mistaken for a sticky bit of romantic drivel until that association is revealed near the poem's close, muting the sentimental gesture. The decasyllabic lines mean to urge the poem forward, both vertically and horizontally, their cadences inexorable, while the threat of imminent violence is mitigated by the leap from Romania to New England, that brief opening of landscape and promise that becomes, with the book's absence, suddenly and cruelly impossible, until the evocative prose of another novel braces the girl.

I revised this poem during the act of composition, rather than taking it through one complete draft, then another, then another. . . . Revision often reveals how craft and luck seduce each other. "I have never started a poem yet whose end I knew," Robert Frost stated in an interview, and Theodore Roethke expressed the same inchoate method in iambic pentameter, his own ten syllables advising what perhaps remains the best approach to writing a poem: "I learn by going where I have to go."

Patricia Jabbeh Wesley

Leaving

Today, Gee shows me what it means to pick up and leave.
Boxes on top of boxes, where a shoe lace refuses to stay

in a teenager's moving-away storage. "Mom," he says,
"the next time we move away to a new town, find

a new church for singing and clapping and youth groups
where everyone cares where you're going when you

have to leave. Talk to someone please, Mom, talk to
someone who knows someone in the new church, in

that new town, and in that neighborhood so there is
someone to speak to when I arrive, and when I have

to leave, so there will be someone I can leave behind."
Sometimes, night can be like that, you see, the invisible

act, the disappearing people we are, when like dark
shadows or the moon and the fire flies, suddenly, we are

no longer there, and yet no one wonders. In another few
days, we will be gone from this small town of unfamiliar

people who never knew we were even passing through
like this. In Byron Center, where we used to live—that

small Michigan Dutch town of small houses, a church
here, a church there, kind people with old stories of having

arrived on ships in the World War. A town where no one
ever went anywhere because now, they all belonged.

My next door neighbor's father used to own his house
before him, after his great grandfather died, leaving

him the house. Small town, small secrets, huge memories,
where the ground is hardened not by anger alone. I am

that other stranger seeking to find roots and ground
and a place where even the squirrel can run free, where

the squirrel also belongs to me. War is such a mystery,
such an unexplained phenomenon, an unexplained

grassland, the indefensible stories of seekers. But no one
clings to those seeking that new homeland, where

memory can find place again. Outside my house, people
refuse to take on to the newcomer or see or ask questions.

They made their friends long ago while I was still in
the Liberian war or before I was even born. So when

I move away tomorrow, I will leave behind only a house
on a bare street corner, where flowers bloom not just

in the spring, a place where the cherry tree at my
front yard blooms pink petals every spring and sheds

them thoughtlessly with rain, and the green lawn across
the road sits quietly, and the neighbors, mute as death.

The Golden Retriever barks all night long, as the cricket
loses track of its own singing. Big mounds of iron hills

rolling, and the neighbor woman's child presses her nose
against the window pane, my invisible neighbor.

I am leaving behind no one at all, don't get me wrong;
this is the new life where only the ghost lives. I am the

blessed one with just one small daughter and a son, a
husband, another son, and another daughter, taken

by the wind. Someone once asked me why people like us
move around so much; why can't we balance feet between

the hills and the sloping crevasses of this new life, between
these old cliffs and the valleys, and I say, "I do not know."

A Poem for Gee

LEAVING TO FIND PLACE IN THE MAKING OF A POEM

This poem, like many other poems I have written, was inspired by the feeling
of displacement, dislocation, and the search for home after the loss of one's
original homeland. It is a poem taken out of real life, inspired, of course, by
my son, Gee, who was not so excited about moving away to a new town just
two years after he had settled in the small town of Indiana, Pennsylvania. He
was beginning to connect, but like the immigrants we are, we were still seek-
ing a place where we could settle down as a family, having moved around for
many years during the Liberian civil war and after we arrived here in the
United States.

But like many of my other poems, the poem is more than a poem about
my life or about my son, Gee, or about his feelings of loss. It is a poem about
the human need to belong, the need to find acceptance, about the feeling of

finding a place where "the squirrel also belongs to me." I believe that a poem is not a poem unless it transcends its original subject matter, its original vision, to become in itself a larger-than-life image, something beyond its author or itself. So, in this poem, the story of the human need to belong, the need to find home, to connect to a world outside of oneself overtakes the poem's original purpose.

Another thing that is important to how I see poetry is my belief that a poem must explore the world from the poet's worldview and from the poet's contextualization of reality or unreality. Here, my worldview about what living in a neighborhood means to me clashes with what I see around me. I come from a culture that is not so mute, where not just the cherry tree sheds its petals thoughtlessly. It is from this perspective or context that I write this poem. In other words, the poem says to the reader: "Here I am, a different kind of person who must survive in a world that is so mute and invisible, a world that makes itself invisible by making me invisible." So the larger context of the poem explores the cultural muteness of neighbors or the invisibility with which I am treated as an individual. Therefore, the poem explores the cultural clashes that the poet must navigate both within the images of the poem and within the world in which the poet lives.

Finally, like most poets I know, I believe that a poet lives on experience, and often that experience exists within the world of the poet's immediate family. Therefore, the inspiration for this poem comes from that source, the family. I know that when I draw upon such experiences, the audience that is so important to my creative process will relate to the poem. Most parents who have had the experience of moving their family, whether within their original homeland or not, can relate to my exploration of my child's feelings because this is the reality of living. I believe that a poem should be relevant to its audience if it is to be relevant to contemporary poetry anywhere.

Katharine Whitcomb

How Flatterers Must Be Shunned

in May your almond trees flung
armfuls of wild perfume at the moon all night
and we could drink the scent through the kitchen window-
screen like stream water, the blossoms' incandescence
hooded until daylight when I would drive home
stunned as someone who's seen a powerful movie
that reminded them of beauty,
pictures replaying as I rolled through the desert
rewinding until I fell asleep in my own bed alone
and dreamed of ribbon-trimmed dresses blowing
on a summer clothesline.

in the beginning you phoned me to discuss God
and I said let's go down that road and don't worry
if it narrows to one lane we'll be fine
but when I thought you might speak you plucked a toothpick
from the ashtray; you turned the radio on.

deer in the yard live almost tame. your dog rested
tethered to a post on grass littered with petals.
the fawns knew her and did not flee. everything
belonged to you. even that honeyed air arcing over us
smelled like your hair after a bath dampening a cotton pillowcase.
how wary and worn out we were back then
when May released your young blooming trees.

THE PRINCE'S ALMOND TREES:
"HOW FLATTERERS MUST BE SHUNNED"

The poet has chosen to use third person in this essay to relieve the weight of the "I."

The poem's title comes from Chapter XXIII in some translations of *The Prince* by Niccolo Machiavelli.

The title has also been translated as "How to Avoid Flatterers."

To use this as the title of a poem that explores the erosion of a love affair is intentionally coy.

The speaker of the poem addresses a "you."

In the poem, "you" owns almond trees. In bloom.

"You" is a dentist the poet met online.

Courts are always full of flatterers.

"You" lives in Idaho still, perhaps. The poet does not know for sure.

The poem is set in May. The poet tries to remember which year.

The poem was written in October after the poet had left "you."

In the poem the blossoms glow like candles.

One must employ terrorism or kindness, as the case dictates.

"You" employed both.

The poet loved the dentist's dog much more than she loved the dentist.

She did not, in fact, ever love the dentist.

"You" courted her first with phone calls about the nature of religion.

Severity is usually more effective, but humanity, in some situations, brings better fruit.

As a child, the poet loved a book illustrated with watercolors by Tasha Tudor.

The phone calls were insufferable. She leaned toward them nevertheless.

Reader: if you are a literalist, events in the poem are true.

Religion must be fostered even though it may be false, provided it is a kind that preserves social solidarity and promotes manly virtues.

"You" spoke at length about Buddhism.

The poet's favorite illustration depicts a little girl hanging sheets on a clothesline in the wind. The caption beneath reads *warm, beautiful summer.*

"You" is not a Buddhist.

Do what you must do in any case, but try to represent it as a special favor to the people.

The little girl's dress blows behind her and the ties on the dress float upward.

"You"'s house is set back off the road between old pastures. Deer love to sleep under his pine trees.

The character Ingrid Fleming in Louis Malle's film *Damage* beats herself with a knotted dishtowel when she discovers the truth about her husband.

If you must commit a crime do not advertise it beforehand.

The poet had never seen almond trees before.

The phone calls prompted her to visit "you" in Idaho.

While writing the poem, she remembered the smell of the trees and the long drive to get there and to get home again.

In person "you" was not so talkative. "You" could not think his way out of a box.

She remembered *The Prince* and those little watercolors.

The poet was loath to dismiss "you" and his startling trees in spite of herself.

This is not a flattering revelation.

"You" became the poet's knotted towel for a while.

Reader: if you are a literalist, we are done.

She made those journeys between Washington and Idaho thinking about Machiavelli, Louis Malle, Tasha Tudor, the wheatfields, the desert, and not "you."

Men should either be caressed or annihilated; appeasement and neutralism are always fatal.

"You" understood power.

There was only one almond tree.

That October she wrote "everything belonged to you" and by then she was long gone.

Note: The italicized lines in this essay are taken from Isaiah Berlin's summaries of the axioms in *The Prince* in his essay "The Question of Machiavelli," first published in the *New York Review of Books*, November 4, 1971.

Robert Wrigley

A Lock of Her Hair

As a hoodoo-voodoo, get-you-back-to-me tool,
this hank's thankless task is vast,
a head down to the ground impossibility, possibly,
since what I'm thinking of is your toe pad pinknesses too,
your soup hots and round-and-rounds, the fine
and perfect poundage of you on my paws, the very cause
and problem I moan and bemoan
the absence of. For Love, above the head
this reddish coil once lavishly wore, there's an air so far away
it's sad for me to even think the same sun's rays play
where it was and do to you what I would do
if I were there or you were here. Still, some thrills
remembered do resemble thrills, one hopes, and the ropes
of it that gently fell around me bound me so well
no hell of miles can defile this dream I dream. I mean
the anyway DNA I can find of you. I mean the home
of bones and blood that holds the whole of you
and which this fizzed-up missive means to conjure, missy,
my world in a curl, girl, this man oh man half man I am
when you're gone.

THE CHARM BY WHICH I MEANT TO BRING HER BACK

Before my wife's hair was short and silver white and radiant, it was long and
auburn and radiant. That I adored it long and dark does not mean I miss it

185

that way now. Not at all. But when I came across a story in the newspaper about a display of locks of various actresses' hair (an exhibition I haven't any interest in), what I suddenly realized was that I could have, years ago, saved a curl, a slender swag, a lock of my lover's hair, and that if I had, it would be a very dear thing to me now, a sort of nineteenth-century-style, late twentieth-century memento. A keepsake, a romantic talisman.

The fact that I didn't have such a lock didn't bother me that much though because what I found most compelling was not the hair itself but a reason to make a poem and, in that way, to do what I didn't do years ago, as well as have what I do not have now. Such is the good fortune of the poet; it's not simply that he can stop time in a lyric but roll it back and revise it as well. So there I was, a day or so after reading the article, examining minutely an imaginary curl of her hair and trying to find a way into a poem.

The challenge I had to contend with in the writing of the poem was as usual twofold: first, what was its point, the particular truth it might seek? And second, what sort of form, structure, and craft would be best suited to engage with that truth? Ordinarily, I operate from number two first, which is to say that I tinker and draft and work the sound of things, the rhythms of things, until the poem's point and truth begin to emerge.

But the problem I kept running into was this: what else would a lock of hair be but a remembrance? And since there she was in my life every day, the memory I found myself celebrating was less my wife's presence *then* than her more youthful self. Not a good plan, I realized, if I ever intended to show her the poem. And besides, it wasn't true. If I missed anyone's younger days, they were my own. So, although it took me a little while to see it, eventually I realized that this lock of hair had to serve a purpose other than the traditional one of remembrance. It could not be only a memento. It had to be that talisman, a charm. But of what, I wondered? What sort of conjuring could I hope to do using a lock of her hair?

Around this time my wife, who is a novelist and memoirist, was traveling quite a bit on a book tour, and I missed her terribly when she was gone. Therefore that lock of imaginary hair became, in the poem at least, my long-distance connection to her and ultimately the method and the charm by which I meant to bring her back to me as soon as I could.

It's an old lesson, of course. Form follows function, and if what I meant to build was a poem that was also a charm, it would have to sound like one. I won't say that it all came easily then; it didn't, but because the challenge was from that point on primarily musical and syntactical, it was, line by line, a lot of hard work I enjoyed. I tinkered with end rhymes for a while, with a certain sort of repeated-line, villanelle structure, but I needed more rhymes than the ends of lines afforded me. And I needed fewer repetitions and a whole lot more gongs.

186

What I hit on is probably as close as I'll ever get to a species of scat, or even rap. I set out trying to see if I could get two or three rhymes in each line, and if not whole rhymes then half ones, as well as all manner of alliteration and assonance. Abracadabras and toils and troubles, so to speak. At first, the poem—through its various drafts around twenty lines long—was one elaborate sentence, which also seemed to me appropriate for a conjuring charm. But without a drum machine and someone going *skreeka-skreeka* on a turntable, I found I just didn't have enough breath to get all the way through the poem smoothly when I read it aloud. The poem had to be pell-mell, had to have an incantatory headlong rhythm; but like most poems, it had an argument to make, and this argument needed variety in its syntax.

With the poem more or less in its final form, I set about finding ways to cleave it into the right number of sentences. What eventually happened was this: the opening sentence is the longest, nearly eight lines. It had to be the longest, it seemed to me. Its job was to pull the reader into both the charm and into the poem's rhetorical strategy. The second and third sentences—four-and-a-half-and three-and-a-half lines respectively—were shorter and thus tightened and focused the poem's syntactical movement. The fourth sentence is barely a single line. The fact that its opening subject and verb rhyme with the final subject and verb clause of the sentence that precedes it (and on the same line) is the means by which I meant to keep the sonic momentum going even as the short sentence's rhetorical intensification occurs. The stops are there, but the pauses are never long. The final sentence—four-and-a-half lines—goes back to the syntactic length of the middle ones, and the short concluding line, the shortest in the poem, asserts the poem's very point and truth, the reason for it.

The poem is great fun to read aloud. A rhyme like "anyway DNA" is just fun to say, and certain suggestive sorts of images, by which I mean those "soup hots and round and rounds," have, I like to believe, a good deal more playful power than anything more overtly sensual. And yes, in truth, I do wish I had a lock of her hair, but as long as this commentary is not attached to the poem everywhere it goes, no one will know that I don't.

JAN BEATTY'S new book, *Red Sugar*, was published by the University of Pittsburgh Press in 2008. Her other books include *Boneshaker* (University of Pittsburgh Press, 2002) and *Mad River*, winner of the 1994 Agnes Lynch Starrett Prize from the University of Pittsburgh Press. *Boneshaker* was a finalist for the Milton Kessler Award, and *Mad River* was a finalist in The Great Lakes Colleges Association Award for New Writing. *Ravenous*, her limited edition chapbook, won the 1995 State Street Prize. Beatty's poetry has appeared in such journals as *Quarterly West, Gulf Coast, Indiana Review, Court Green*, as well as in anthologies published by Oxford University Press, University of Illinois Press, and University of Iowa Press. Beatty has worked as a welfare caseworker, an abortion counselor, in maximum security prisons, and as a waitress for fifteen years. Her awards include the $15,000 Creative Achievement Award in Literature from the Heinz Foundation, the Pablo Neruda Prize for Poetry, and two fellowships from the Pennsylvania Council on the Arts. For the past thirteen years, she has hosted and produced *Prosody*, a public radio show on NPR-affiliate WYEP-FM featuring the work of national writers. Beatty directs the creative writing program at Carlow University, where she runs the Madwomen in the Attic writing workshops and teaches in the MFA program.

ROBIN BECKER'S books in the Pitt Poetry Series include *Domain of Perfect Affection* (2006), *The Horse Fair* (2000), *All-American Girl* (1996), and *Giacometti's Dog* (1990). The Frick Art and Historical Center in Pittsburgh printed her chapbook *Venetian Blue* in 2002. Professor of English at Pennsylvania State University, Becker has received fellowships from the Bunting Institute, the Massachusetts Cultural Council, and the National Endowment for the Arts. She serves as Poetry Editor for *Women's Review of Books* and writes a column for the *WRB* on poetry and the poetry scene called "Field Notes."

FLEDA BROWN won the Felix Pollak Prize for her newest collection of poems, *Reunion* (University of Wisconsin Press, 2007). She is the author of five previous collections, most recently *The Women Who Loved Elvis All Their*

189

Lives (Carnegie Mellon University Press, 2004). Her others are *Fishing With Blood* (winner of the Great Lakes Colleges New Writer's Award, Purdue University Press, 1988), *Do Not Peel the Birches* (Purdue, 1993), *The Devil's Child* (Carnegie Mellon University Press, 1999), and *Breathing In, Breathing Out*, (winner of the Philip Levine Prize, Anhinga Press, 2002). A collection of memoir essays, *Driving With Dvorak*, is forthcoming from the University of Nebraska Press. She is retired from the University of Delaware and is on the faculty of the Rainier Writing Workshop, a low-residency MFA program at Pacific Lutheran University. She is a former poet laureate of Delaware.

J. L. CONRAD'S poems have appeared in *Columbia: A Journal of Literature and Art, Third Coast, Beloit Poetry Journal, H_NGM_N, Southeast Review, Phoebe, Alligator Juniper* and *Cream City Review.. A Cartography of Birds*, her first collection of poems, was published in 2002 by Louisiana State University Press. She is currently working toward her Ph.D. in Literary Studies at the University of Wisconsin-Madison.

JIM DANIELS is the winner of the Blue Lynx Poetry Prize for his book *Revolt of the Crash Test Dummies* (Eastern Washington University Press, 2007). Two other of his books were also published in 2007; his third collection of short fiction, *Mr. Pleasant* (Michigan State University Press), and his eleventh book of poems, *In Line for the Exterminator* (Wayne State University Press). In 2005, Jim Daniels wrote and produced the independent film *Dumpster*, which appeared in more than a dozen film festivals, and published *Street* (Bottom Dog Press), a book of his poems accompanying the photographs of Charlee Brodsky. He is a recipient of the Tillie Olsen Prize, the Brittingham Prize for Poetry, two fellowships from the National Endowment for the Arts, and two fellowships from the Pennsylvania Council on the Arts. His poems have appeared in the Pushcart Prize and Best American Poetry anthologies. He is the Thomas Stockman Baker Professor of English at Carnegie Mellon University, where he directs the Creative Writing Program.

TODD DAVIS, winner of the Gwendolyn Brooks Poetry Prize, teaches creative writing, environmental studies, and American literature at Pennsylvania State University's Altoona College. His poems have been nominated for the Pushcart Prize and have appeared in such journals and magazines as *North American Review, Iowa Review, Indiana Review, Gettysburg Review, West Branch, River Styx, Arts & Letters, Quarterly West, Green Mountains Review, Poetry East, Nebraska Review,* and *Image.* He is the author of three books of poems, *The Least of These* (Michigan State University Press, 2010), *Some Heaven* (Michigan State University Press, 2007) and *Ripe* (Bottom Dog

190

Press, 2002). His work has been featured on the radio by Garrison Keillor on *The Writer's Almanac* and by Marion Roach on *The Naturalist's Datebook*, as well as by Ted Kooser in his syndicated newspaper column *American Life in Poetry*. In addition to his creative work, Davis is the author or editor of six scholarly books, including *Kurt Vonnegut's Crusade, or How a Postmodern Harlequin Preached a New Kind of Humanism* (State University of New York Press, 2006) and *Mapping the Ethical Turn: A Reader in Ethics, Culture, and Literary Theory* (University Press of Virginia, 2001).

CHRIS DOMBROWSKI is the author of a chapbook of poems, *Fragments with Dusk in Them* (Punctilious Press), and a full-length collection, *By Cold Water* (Wayne State University Press, 2009). His work has appeared in *Colorado Review*, *Crazyhorse*, *Denver Quarterly*, *Orion*, and *Poetry*. He has worked as a riverguide, poet-in-the-schools, and teacher of creative writing at Interlochen Center for the Arts and the University of Montana in Missoula, where he lives with his family.

DAN GERBER is a poet, novelist, and writer of nonfiction who has worked as a professional racing driver, a corporate executive, and a high school and university teacher. He has been nominated for two Pushcart Prizes, won the 1992 Michigan Author Award, and had his work included in *The Best American Poetry 1999*. In 2001 he received the Mark Twain Award for distinguished contributions to Midwestern Literature. His books include *The Revenant* (1971), *Departure* (1973), *American Atlas* (1973), *Out of Control* (1974), *The Chinese Poems* (1978), *Snow on the Backs of Animals* (1986), *Grass Fires* (1987), *A Voice from the River* (1990), *A Last Bridge Home: New and Selected Poems* (1992), *Trying To Catch the Horses* (1999), which won the *ForeWord Magazine* Book of the Year Award in Poetry, and *A Second Life: Collected Nonfiction* (2001). His poems and stories have appeared in *Nation*, *The New Yorker*, *Sports Illustrated*, *Playboy*, *New Letters*, *Fourth Genre*, *Poetry*, and *Georgia Review*.. From 1968 through 1972, with Jim Harrison, he co-edited the literary magazine *Sumac*.

JEFF GUNDY is Professor of English at Bluffton University in Ohio. He is the author of three collections of nonfiction: *A Community of Memory: My Days with George and Clara* (University of Illinois Press), *Scattering Point: The World in a Mennonite Eye* (SUNY Press), and *Walker in the Fog: On Mennonite Writing* (Cascadia Publishing House). Gundy has also published five books of poetry: *Spoken Among the Trees* (University of Akron Press, 2007), *Deerflies* (WordTech Editions), *Rhapsody with Dark Matter* (Bottom Dog Press), *Flatlands* (Cleveland State University Press), and *Inquiries* (Bottom Dog Press).

191

KIMIKO HAHN is the author of eight collections of poetry, including *The Unbearable Heart*, which received an American Book Award; *Earshot*, a Theodore Roethke Memorial Prize, and an Association of Asian American Studies Award; *The Narrow Road to the Interior* (W.W. Norton, 2006); and *Toxic Flora* (forthcoming from W.W. Norton, 2010). She has also written for film; the latest, *Everywhere at Once*, was narrated by Jeanne Moreau and presented at The Cannes Film Festival. Her fellowships include those from The National Endowment for the Arts, the Lila Wallace-Reader's Digest Foundation, and the Shelley Memorial Prize. She teaches in the MFA Program at Queens College, The City University of New York.

WILLIAM HEYEN was born in Brooklyn, New York, in 1940. He is Professor of English and Poet-in-Residence Emeritus at SUNY Brockport. He has received Fulbright, Guggenheim, NEA, American Academy and Institute of Arts and Letters, and other awards. Among his books, *Noise in the Trees* (1974) was an American Library Association "Notable Book"; *Crazy Horse in Stillness* (1996) won the Small Press Book Award for Poetry in 1997; and *Shoah Train: Poems* (2004) was a finalist for the National Book Award.

H. L. HIX teaches at the University of Wyoming. His recent books include a collection of essays on poetry, *As Easy As Lying*; an anthology, *Wild and Whirling Words*; two poetry collections, *Legible Heavens* and *Chromatic*, a finalist for the 2006 National Book Award; *and God Bless*, a "political/poetic discourse" built around sonnets and sestinas and villanelles composed of quotations from George W. Bush. All are published by Etruscan Press.

JOHN HOPPENTHALER received his MFA from Virginia Commonwealth University in 1988. His poetry has appeared in *Ploughshares, Southern Review, Virginia Quarterly Review, McSweeney's Internet Tendency, Laurel Review*, and *Blackbird*, as well as in the anthologies *September 11, 2001: American Writers Respond, Poetry Calendar, Chance of a Ghost, Blooming through the Ashes*, and *Wild, Sweet Notes II: More West Virginia Poetry*. For eleven years he served as Poetry Editor for *Kestrel*; he now serves as advisory editor for the cultural journal *Connotation Press: An Online Artifact*, where he also edits "A Poetry Congeries" and curates a guest-edited poetry feature. He has been the recipient of an Individual Artist Grant from the West Virginia Commission on the Arts, as well as residency fellowships to the MacDowell Colony, the Virginia Center for the Arts, and the Weymouth Center for the Humanities. His books of poetry are *Lives of Water* (2003) and *Anticipate the Coming Reservoir* (2008), both with Carnegie Mellon University Press. He teaches creative writing and literature at East Carolina University.

ANN HOSTETLER is the author of *Empty Room with Light* (Pandora Press, 2002) and the editor of *A Cappella: Mennonite Voices in Poetry* (University of Iowa Press, 2003). Her essays and poems have appeared in such places as *PMLA*, *American Scholar*, and *Cream City Review*, as well as numerous anthologies. Recently she served on the editorial team of *Letters from the World: Poems from the Wom-po Listserv* (Red Hen Press, 2008). She is a Professor of English and Creative Writing at Goshen College, in Goshen, Indiana, where she lives with her family.

JULIA SPICHER KASDORF has published two books of poetry, *Sleeping Preacher*, winner of the Agnes Lynch Starrett Poetry Prize from the University of Pittsburgh Press, and *Eve's Striptease*. She has also authored a book of essays, *The Body and the Book: Writing from a Mennonite Life*, and a biography, *Fixing Tradition: Joseph W. Yoder, Amish American*. With Michael Tyrell, she edited *Broken Land: Poems of Brooklyn*. She teaches creative writing at The Pennsylvania State University.

DAVID KIRBY is the Robert O. Lawton Distinguished Professor of English at Florida State University. *The House on Boulevard St.: New and Selected Poems* was a National Book Award Finalist in 2007. His latest collection is *The Temple Gate Called Beautiful* (Alice James Books, 2008).

GERRY LaFEMINA'S latest book is *The Book of Clown Baby/ Figures from the Big Time Circus Book* (Mayapple Press, 2007). His other books include *The Parakeets of Brooklyn* (Bordighera Press, 2004) and *The Window Facing Winter* (New Issues Press, 2004). The co-editor of *Review Revue*, an independent journal of reviews, prosody essays, and interviews with poets, LaFemina directs the Frostburg Center for Creative Writing at Frostburg State University where he also teaches.

MARY LINTON is a wetland ecologist and aquatic biologist. Linton's special interest is aquatic communities, particularly amphibians, dragonflies and damselflies, and aquatic beetles. As far as she is concerned, a day swimming in a crystal clear lake, wading the riffles and pools of a northern trout stream, or mucking about a fertile wetland could not be better spent. Mary Linton's ecological articles have appeared in *Evolution, Ecology, Evolutionary Ecology, Canadian Entomology, Herpetological Review, American Naturalist*, and *Proceedings of the Indiana Academy of Sciences*, as well as popular magazines. Her poetry has appeared in *Appalachia, Aethlon, Blueline, Builder, Country Feedback Magazine, Poetry Motel*, and *Seeding the Snow*.

SHARA MCCALLUM has published two books of poems, *Song of Thieves* (University of Pittsburgh Press, 2003) and *The Water Between Us* (University of Pittsburgh Press, 1999), a winner of the 1998 Agnes Lynch Starrett Poetry Prize. Her poems and personal essays have appeared in numerous literary journals and been reprinted in over twenty anthologies of American, African American, Caribbean, and world poetry. Originally from Jamaica, McCallum directs the Stadler Center for Poetry and teaches at Bucknell University. She is also on the faculty of the Stonecoast Low Residency MFA program. She lives in Pennsylvania with her family.

DINTY W. MOORE is the author of *Between Panic and Desire, The Accidental Buddhist, Toothpick Men, The Emperor's Virtual Clothes*, and the writing guide, *The Truth of the Matter: Art and Craft in Creative Nonfiction*. He has published essays and stories in *Southern Review, Georgia Review, Harpers, New York Times Sunday Magazine, Utne Reader*, and *Crazyhorse*. He teaches writing at Ohio University.

ERIN MURPHY is the author of three collections of poetry: *Dislocation and Other Theories* (Word Press, 2008); *Too Much of This World* (Mammoth Books, 2008), winner of the Anthony Piccione Poetry Prize; and *Science of Desire* (Word Press, 2004), a finalist for the Paterson Poetry Prize. Her awards include the National Writers' Union Poetry Award judged by Donald Hall, a Dorothy Sargent Rosenberg Poetry Prize, the Foley Poetry Award, and fellowships from the Pennsylvania Council on the Arts, the Maryland State Arts Council, and the Virginia Center for the Creative Arts. Her poems have appeared in dozens of journals and in several anthologies, including *180 More: Extraordinary Poems for Every Day*, edited by Billy Collins. She is on the faculty at Pennsylvania State University's Altoona College, where she teaches English and creative writing.

MARY ROSE O'REILLEY is the author of *The Barn at the End of the World: The Apprenticeship of a Quaker, Buddhist Shepherd, The Peaceable Classroom, Radical Presence*, and *Half Wild: Poems*, winner of the Walt Whitman Award for Poetry. Her recent awards include a Minnesota State Arts Board Grant, a Bush Artist's Fellowship, a Loft Mentor grant in poetry, a Sears Roebuck Foundation Award for Campus Leadership and Excellence in Teaching, and a Helen Hole Fellowship for Quaker Teachers. She taught English at the University of St. Thomas in St. Paul, Minnesota, from 1978–2006.

LEE PETERSON'S *Rooms and Fields: Dramatic Monologues from the War in Bosnia* was the Winner of the 2003 Stan and Tom Wick Poetry Prize from

194

Kent State University Press. Her poems have appeared in such journals as *North American Review, Nimrod, Runes, Comstock Review*, and *Seattle Review*. She has held the position of emerging writer-in-residence at Pennsylvania State University's Altoona College and currently teaches there.

GREG RAPPLEYE is corporation counsel for Ottawa County, Grand Haven, Michigan. He's the author of three poetry collections—*Figured Dark* (University of Arkansas Press, 2007), *A Path Between Houses* (University of Wisconsin Press, 2000), and *Holding Down the Earth* (SkyBooks, 1995)—as well as two chapbooks. A past Bread Loaf Fellow in poetry, he has won a number of awards, including a Pushcart Prize, the Paumanok Poetry Award, and the Brittingham Prize, and he was the first runner-up for the 2007 Dorset Prize.

KEITH RATZLAFF'S books of poetry are *Then, a Thousand Crows; Dubious Angels: Poems after Paul Klee; Man Under A Pear Tree;* and *Across The Known World.* His poems and reviews have appeared in *Cincinnati Review, Georgia Review, The Journal, New England Review, Threepenny Review, Arts and Letters, Colorado Review,* and *North American Review.* His recent poems and essays also appear in *Poets of the New Century* (David R. Godine, 2001); *A Cappella: Mennonite Voices in Poetry* (University of Iowa Press, 2003); *In the Middle of the Middle West: Literary Nonfiction from the Heartland* (Indiana University Press, 2003); *Snakebird: Thirty Years of Anhinga Poets* (Anhinga Press, 2004), and in *The Best American Poetry* 2009 (Scribner, 2009). His awards include the Anhinga Prize for Poetry, the Theodore Roethke Award, and a Pushcart Prize. He teaches writing and literature at Central College in Pella, Iowa.

JACK RIDL'S most recent collections are *Losing Season* (CavanKerry Press, 2009) and *Broken Symmetry* (Wayne State Universtiy Press, 2006). He is the author of two other full-length collections, three chapbooks (*Outside the Center Ring*, a collection of circus poems is the most recent), and a compilation volume assembled from the previous collections. In 2001, his collection *Against Elegies* was selected by Sharon Dolin and former U.S. Poet Laureate Billy Collins for the 2001 Chapbook Award from The Center for Book Arts in New York City. Ridl, who taught at Hope College for thirty-six years and who founded the college's Visiting Writers Series, is coauthor with Peter Schakel of *Approaching Poetry* (Bedford/St. Martin's) and co-editor (with Peter Schakel) of both *250 Poems* and *Literature: A Portable Anthology*, also from Bedford/St. Martin's. Their *Approaching Literature in the 21st Century* was published by Bedford/St. Martin's in 2005.

STEVEN SHERRILL earned an MFA in poetry from the Iowa Writers' Workshop and received a National Endowment for the Arts Fellowship for Fiction in 2002. His poems and stories have appeared in *The Best American Poetry*, *Kenyon Review*, *River Styx*, and *Georgia Review*, among others. He is the author of a book of poems, *Ersatz Anatomy*, forthcoming from Custom Words Press, as well as the novels *The Minotaur Takes a Cigarette Break* (John F. Blair, 2000), *Visits from the Drowned Girl* (Random House, 2004), and *The Locktender's House* (Random House, 2008).

DAVID SHUMATE lives in Zionsville, Indiana. His prose poems have appeared widely in literary journals including *North American Review*, *Mid-American Review*, *Mississippi Review*, *Maize*, *Southern Indiana Review*, and *Prairie Schooner*. He is the author of two books, *The Floating Bridge* (University of Pittsburgh Press, 2008) and *High Water Mark* (University of Pittsburgh Press, 2004), which was awarded the 2003 Agnes Lynch Starrett prize and received first place in the poetry category of the "Best Books of Indiana" competition of 2005. His work has also been featured on Garrison Keillor's *The Writer's Almanac* and in Keillor's *Good Poems for Hard Times*.

AARON SMITH is the author of *Blue on Blue Ground* (Pittsburgh, 2005), winner of the Agnes Lynch Starrett Poetry Prize. His chapbook, *What's Required* (Thorngate Road, 2003), won the Frank O'Hara Award. His work has appeared in various publications, including *Barrow Street, Court Green, 5 AM, Gulf Coast, Pleiades,* and *Prairie Schooner.* He is a 2007 Fellow in Poetry from the New York Foundation for the Arts.

LUCIEN STRYK, poet and translator, has won numerous awards and fellowships, including a National Endowment for the Arts Poetry Fellowship, a Rockefeller Foundation Fellowship, a Ford Foundation Fellowship, a Fulbright grant and lectureship, and a National Institute of Arts and Letters award. The author, translator, or editor of over thirty books of poetry, Stryk's most recent books include *And Still Birds Sing: New and Collected Poems* (1998), *The Gift of Great Poetry* (1992), *Of Pen and Ink and Paper Scraps* (1989), and *Bells of Lombardy* (1986).

MARY SWANDER, Poet Laureate of Iowa, is also the author of three books of nonfiction, *The Desert Pilgrim* (Viking, 2003), *Out of this World: A Woman's Life among the Amish* (Viking, 1995), and *Parsnips in the Snow* (with Jane Staw, University of Iowa Press, 1990). Her books of poetry include, *Heaven-and-Earth House* (Alfred Knopf, 1994), *Driving the Body Back* (Alfred Knopf, 1986), and *Succession* (University of Georgia Press, 1979), as well as the forth-

196

coming *The Girls on the Roof* (Turning Point Press). Swander is Distinguished University Professor of English at Iowa State University and lives in Ames and Kalona, Iowa, where she raises sheep and goats and a large organic vegetable garden.

SUE ELLEN THOMPSON is the author of *This Body of Silk*, which won the 1986 Samuel French Morse Prize, *The Wedding Boat* (Owl Creek Press), as well as *The Leaving: New and Selected Poems* and *The Golden Hour*, both published by Autumn House. She is also the editor of *The Autumn House Anthology of Contemporary American Poetry*. She has been a Robert Frost Fellow at the Bread Loaf Writers' Conference, Visiting Writer at Central Connecticut State University, and Poet-in-Residence at SUNY Binghamton and at the Frost place in Franconia, New Hampshire. Her poems have reached a large national audience through Garrison Keillor's *The Writer's Almanac* and Ted Kooser's *American Life in Poetry*. She has received a number of national prizes and has been nominated twice for the Pulitzer, most recently in 2006 for *The Golden Hour*.

NATASHA TRETHEWEY was born in Gulfport, Mississippi, in 1966. She is author of three collections of poetry, *Domestic Work* (Graywolf, 2000), *Bellocq's Ophelia* (Graywolf, 2002), and *Native Guard* (Houghton Mifflin, 2006) for which she won the Pulitzer Prize. At Emory University she is Professor of English and holds the Phillis Wheatley Distinguished Chair in Poetry.

BRIAN TURNER earned an MFA from the University of Oregon and lived abroad in South Korea for a year before serving for seven years in the US Army. He was an infantry team leader for a year in Iraq with the 3rd Stryker Brigade Combat Team, 2nd Infantry Division. *Here, Bullet* (Alice James Books, 2005) was written while Turner served in Iraq. His second book, *Phantom Noise*, is forthcoming from Alice James Books. His poetry has been published in *Poetry Daily*, *Georgia Review*, and other journals. He is the recipient of a 2006 Lannan Literary Fellowship, a 2007 NEA Fellowship in Poetry, and a 2009-10 Amy Lowell Traveling Scholar Fellowship. He is on the faculty of Sierra Nevada College.

LEE UPTON'S fifth book of poetry, *Undid in the Land of Undone*, was published by New Issues Press. Her fourth book of literary criticism, *Defensive Measures*, was published by Bucknell University Press. Her novella, *The Guide to the Flying Island*, appeared in 2009 and was the winner of the Miami University Novella Competition. Her poetry, fiction, and criticism appear widely. She is a professor of English and the writer-in-residence at Lafayette College.

G. C. WALDREP is the author of *Goldbeater's Skin* (Colorado Prize, 2003), *Disclamor* (BOA Editions, 2007), and *Archicembalo* (Tupelo Press, 2009), as well as two chapbooks, "The Batteries" (New Michigan Press, 2006) and "One Way No Exit" (Tarpaulin Sky, 2008). His work has received awards from the Poetry Society of America, the Academy of American Poets, the National Endowment for the Arts, and the Campbell Corner Foundation, as well as a Pushcart Prize. He lives in Lewisburg, Pennsylvania, and teaches at Bucknell University.

MICHAEL WATERS teaches at Monmouth University and in the Drew University MFA Program in Poetry and Poetry in Translation. He is Professor Emeritus at Salisbury University in Maryland. His books of poetry include *Darling Vulgarity* (2006), a finalist for The Los Angeles Times Book Prize); *Parthenopi: New and Selected Poems* (2001), a finalist for the Paterson Poetry Prize; and *Green Ash Red Maple, Black Gum* (1997)—all published by BOA Editions—and *Bountiful* (1992); *The Burden Lifters* (1989); and *Anniversary of the Air* (1985)—all published by Carnegie Mellon University Press. He has also edited several volumes, including *Contemporary American Poetry* (Houghton Mifflin, 2006) and *Perfect in the Their Art: Poems on Boxing from Homer to Ali* (Southern Illinois University Press, 2003). The recipient of a fellowship in creative writing from the National Endowment for the Arts, Individual Artist Awards from the Maryland State Arts Council, and four Pushcart Prizes, he has taught at Ohio University and the University of Maryland, and has been Visiting Professor of American Literature at the University of Athens, Greece, as well as Banister Writer-in-Residence at Sweet Briar College, Stadler Poet-in-Residence at Bucknell University, Distinguished Poet-in-Residence at Wichita State University, and Fulbright Scholar in American Studies at Al. I Cuza University in Iasi, Romania.

PATRICIA JABBEH WESLEY, who immigrated from Liberia with her family during the Liberian civil war, is the author of two books of poetry, *Before The Palm Could Bloom: Poems of Africa* (New Issues Press, 1998) and *Becoming Ebony* (Southern Illinois University Press, 2003). Her work has appeared in many literary journals and magazines, including, *Poets of Africa: Echoes Across the Valley*, an Anthology of African poetry, *New Orleans Review, Crab Orchard Review, Cortland Review,* and *Newsday*.She teaches creative writing and English at Pennsylvania State University's Altoona College.

KATHARINE WHITCOMB was born in Appleton, Wisconsin, and earned her BA from Macalester College in English. In 1995 she received an MFA in Writing from Vermont College of Norwich University. She is the author of a collection of poems, *Saints of South Dakota & Other Poems*, which was chosen

198

by Lucia Perillo as the winner of the 2000 Bluestem Award and published by Bluestem Press. Her poetry awards include a Stegner Fellowship at Stanford University, a Loft-McKnight Award, a Writing Fellowship at the Fine Arts Work Center in Provincetown, and a Halls Fellowship at the Wisconsin Institute for Creative Writing. She received an AWP Fellowship in Poetry to the Prague Summer Seminars at Charles University in the Czech Republic. She has had work published in *Paris Review, Yale Review, Kenyon Review* and *Missouri Review* as well as several anthologies, including *Dorothy Parker's Elbow: Tattoos on Writers, Writers on Tattoos*. She currently coordinates the writing program at Central Washington University.

ROBERT WRIGLEY'S collections of poetry include *Earthly Meditations: New and Selected Poems* (Penguin, 2006); *Lives of the Animals* (Penguin, 2003); *Reign of Snakes* (Penguin, 1999), winner of the Kingsley Tufts Award; *In the Bank of Beautiful Sins* (Penguin, 1995), winner of the San Francisco Poetry Center Book Award and a Lenore Marshall Award finalist; *What My Father Believed* (University of Illinois Press, 1991); *Moon in a Mason Jar* (University of Illinois Press, 1986); and *The Sinking of Clay City* (Copper Canyon Press, 1979). His work has also been published in numerous anthologies and literary journals, including *The New Yorker, Atlantic, Poetry,* and *Kenyon Review.* Wrigley's awards and honors include fellowships from the National Endowment for the Arts, the Idaho State Commission on the Arts, and the Guggenheim Foundation, as well as the J. Howard and Barbara M. J. Wood Prize, the Frederick Bock Prize from *Poetry* magazine, the Wagner Award from the Poetry Society of America, the Theodore Roethke Award from *Poetry Northwest,* and four Pushcart Prizes. From 1986 until 1988 he served as the state of Idaho's writer-in-residence. He currently teaches in the MFA program in creative writing at the University of Idaho.

Acknowledgments

WE ARE GRATEFUL to the authors, editors, and publishers who have given us permission to reprint poems.

We also wish to thank Lori Bechtel-Wherry, Kenneth Womack, Marc Harris, Brian Black, Tom Liszka, KT Huckabee, Ian Marshall, Megan Simpson, Molly Slep, and Stephanie Tanner of Pennsylvania State University, Altoona College; R.C. De Prospo of Washington College; Donna Murphy; Maribeth Fischer; and James Peltz, Gary Dunham, Kelli Williams-LaRoux, Anne Valentine, and Amanda Lanne of State University of New York Press. In addition, we thank the Pennsylvania Council on the Arts and Pennsylvania State University for grants that helped in the completion of this book.

Jan Beatty, "Red Sugar," first appeared in *Red Sugar*, University of Pittsburgh Press, 2008. Reprinted by permission of the author. Copyright 2009 by Jan Beatty.

Robin Becker, "Man of the Year," first appeared in *Domain of Perfect Affection*, University of Pittsburgh Press, 2006. Reprinted by permission of the author. Copyright 2009 by Robin Becker.

Fleda Brown, "Knot Tying Lessons: The Slip Knot," first appeared in *Georgia Review*, No. 58, Summer 2004. Reprinted by permission of the author. Copyright 2009 by Fleda Brown.

Conrad, J. L., "Brother André's Heart: Montreal, 2003." Reprinted by permission of the author. Copyright 2009 by J. L. Conrad.

Daniels, Jim, "Factory Jungle," first appeared in *Places/Everyone*, University of Wisconsin Press, 1985. Reprinted by permission of the author. Copyright 2009 by Jim Daniels.

Todd Davis, "Loving the Flesh," first appeared in *Ripe*, Bottom Dog Press, 2002. "The Body of Poetry" first appeared in *Review Revue* 4.1, 2007. Reprinted by permission of the author. Copyright 2009 by Todd Davis.

Chris Dombrowski, "Elegy with Fall's Last Filaments." Reprinted by permission of the author. Copyright 2009 by Chris Dombrowski.

Dan Gerber, "To W. S. Merwin." Reprinted by permission of the author. Copyright 2009 by Dan Gerber.

Jeff Gundy, "Contemplation with Ledges and Moon," first appeared in *Spoken among the Trees*, University of Akron Press, 2007. Reprinted by permission of the author. Copyright 2009 by Jeff Gundy.

Kimiko Hahn, "Pink," first appeared in *TriQuarterly Review*, No. 122. Reprinted by permission of the author. Copyright 2009 by Kimiko Hahn.

William Heyen, "Longhouse," first appeared in *Amicus Journal* and was collected in *The Rope*, Mammoth Press, 2002. Reprinted by permission of the author. Copyright 2009 by William Heyen.

H. L. Hix, "awash with blushing textures, your hips, lipped lilies." Reprinted by permission of the author. Copyright 2009 by H. L. Hix.

John Hoppenthaler, "Dance," first appeared in *Tar River Poetry*, Spring 2007. Reprinted by permission of the author. Copyright 2009 by John Hoppenthaler.

Ann Hostetler, "Sonnets for the Amish Girls of Nickel Mines," first appeared in *Mennonite Weekly Review*, 1 January 2007. Reprinted by permission of the author. Copyright 2009 by Ann Hostetler.

Julia Spicher Kasdorf, "Double the Digits," first appeared in *Paris Review*, No. 155, Summer 2000. Reprinted by permission of the author. Copyright 2009 by Julia Spicher Kasdorf.

David Kirby, "Borges at the Northside Rotary," first appeared in *The Ha-Ha* (Southern Messenger Poets, 2003) and later in *The House on Boulevard St.: New and Selected Poems* (Southern Messenger Press, 2007). Reprinted by permission of the author. Copyright 2009 by David Kirby.

Gerry LaFemina, "Clown Baby's Summer" and "The Conception of Clown Baby," first appeared in *The Book of Clown Baby/ Figures from the Big Time Circus Book*(Mayapple Press, 2007). Reprinted by permission of the author. Copyright 2009 by Gerry LaFemina.

Mary Linton, "Up Late with Loons." Reprinted by permission of the author. Copyright 2009 by Mary Linton.

Shara McCallum, "Penelope," first appeared in *Antioch Review*, Vol. 62, No. 4, 2004. Reprinted by permission of the author. Copyright 2009 by Shara McCallum.

Dinty Moore, "Revelation." Reprinted by permission of the author. Copyright 2009 by Dinty Moore.

Erin Murphy, "Covetous," first appeared in the June 5-12, 2006 issue of *America* and in *Dislocation and Other Theories* (Word Press, 2008). The poem and a version of "Coveting Thy Neighbor's Poem" appeared in the Spring 2007 online issue of the *Southeast Review*. Both are reprinted by permission of the author. Copyright 2009 by Erin Murphy.

202

Mary Rose O'Reilley, "The Third Winter." Reprinted by permission of the author. Copyright 2009 by Mary Rose O'Reilley.

Lee Peterson, "Anniversary." Reprinted by permission of the author. Copyright 2009 by Lee Peterson.

Greg Rappleye, "Orpheus, Gathering the Trees." Reprinted by permission of the author. Copyright 2009 by Greg Rappleye.

Keith Ratzlaff, "Sunday," first appeared in *Arts & Letters*, No.12, 2004. Reprinted by permission of the author. Copyright 2009 by Keith Ratzlaff.

Jack Ridl, "Repairing the House." Reprinted by permission of the author. Copyright 2009 by Jack Ridl.

Steven Sherrill, "Coming Out of Caliban." Reprinted by permission of the author. Copyright 2009 by Steven Sherrill.

David Shumate, "Revising My Memoirs," first appeared in *Poetry East* 64/65, Spring 2009. Reprinted by permission of the author. Copyright 2009 by David Shumate.

Aaron Smith, "Christopher Street Pier (Summer)," first appeared in *Barrow Street*, Winter 2007. Reprinted by permission of the author. Copyright 2009 by Aaron Smith.

Lucien Stryk, "Blood," first appeared in *American Poetry Review*, May/June 1999. Reprinted by permission of the author. Copyright 2009 by Lucien Stryk.

Mary Swander, "Hot Pads, Cold Pads." Reprinted by permission of the author. Copyright 2009 by Mary Swander.

Sue Ellen Thompson, "Fishing on the Merrimack, My Father Sees a B-24" and "Prisoner of War," first appeared in *The Golden Hour*(Autumn House Press, 2006). Reprinted by permission of the author. Copyright 2009 by Sue Ellen Thompson.

Natasha Trethewey, "Myth," first appeared in *New England Review* 25.4, 2004, and later in *Native Guard* (Houghton Mifflin, 2006). Reprinted by permission of the author. Copyright 2009 by Natasha Trethewey.

Brian Turner, "At the Farmer's Market in Eugene." Reprinted by permission of the author. Copyright 2009 by Brian Turner.

G. C. Waldrep, "Anniversary," first appeared in *Denver Quarterly* 42:1, 2008. Reprinted by permission of the author. Copyright 2009 by G.C. Waldrep.

Lee Upton, "The Weak Already Inherited." Reprinted by permission of the author. Copyright 2009 by Lee Upton.

Michael Waters, "Beloved." Reprinted by permission of the author. Copyright 2009 by Michael Waters.

Patricia Jabbeh Wesley, "Leaving." Reprinted by permission of the author. Copyright 2009 by Patricia Jabbeh Wesley.

Katharine Whitcomb, "How Flatterers Must Be Shunned." Reprinted by permission of the author. Copyright 2009 by Katharine Whitcomb.

Robert Wrigley, "A Lock of Her Hair." Reprinted by permission of the author. Copyright 2009 by Robert Wrigley.